HOW TO
COOK
AND KEEP ON
COOKING

Lincolnshire
COUNTY COUNCIL

discover libraries

This book should be returned on or before the due date.

To renew or order library books please telephone 01522 782010
or visit https://lincolnshire.spydus.co.uk
You will require a Personal Identification Number.
Ask any member of staff for this.

The above does not apply to Reader's Group Collection Stock.

HOW TO
COOK
AND KEEP ON
COOKING

SIMON BOYLE

EBURY
PRESS

1 3 5 7 9 10 8 6 4 2

Published in 2018 by Ebury Press, an imprint of Ebury Publishing,
20 Vauxhall Bridge Road,
London SW1V 2SA

Ebury Press is part of the Penguin Random House group
of companies whose addresses can be found at
global.penguinrandomhouse.com

Copyright © Simon Boyle 2018

Simon Boyle has asserted his right to be identified as the author
of this Work in accordance with the Copyright, Designs and
Patents Act 1988

First published by Ebury Press in 2018

www.penguin.co.uk

A CIP catalogue record for this book is available from
the British Library

ISBN 9781529103267

Original design by Alison O'Toole
Typesetting by Jerry Goldie
Illustrations by Stuart Hounslow

Printed and bound in Italy by L.E.G.O. S.p.A

Penguin Random House is committed to a sustainable future for
our business, our readers and our planet. This book is made from
Forest Stewardship Council® certified paper.

CONTENTS

PART I
BORING STUFF

PART II
DELICIOUS STUFF

FRESH
INGREDIENTS
+
FRIENDS OR FAMILY
=
SHARING +
GOOD HEALTH

Food has played an important role throughout my life. I used to run home from school to peel potatoes for shepherd's pie. I learned to roast chicken at a young age because I loved the juicy flavour of the meat. And I made cakes when I should have been doing my homework. I was lucky that my parents always cooked great food and taught me what they knew.

I carried on cooking when I started an apprenticeship at the Savoy Hotel in London. In my spare time, I cooked for my brothers and friends. These occasions were filled with so much fun, laughter and love that my mantra became all about 'bringing people together through food'.

I built a restaurant business based on this idea later in my career. I also got thinking about people who leave school, fall on hard times and become homeless. In particular, I wondered why people become homeless and stay homeless in this day and age. As I've got older, I've had my own children and I've worked with everyone from vulnerable adults to working professionals. It has made me realise that food plays a vital role in each and every one of our lives. But not everyone has had the opportunity to learn about food from their parents, grandparents or at school.

As a result, I created a charity to help tackle the issue of people spiralling into homelessness when they don't have the right skills or support to fall back on. Food can and does help change lives. Ultimately, good food provides the right energy and motivation for you to look after yourself and succeed.

I wrote this book to help people start off on their own. Maybe you can't cook or are not at all confident in the kitchen. Whether you're leaving school, are off to university, getting your first home, starting a new relationship, beginning your career or simply never needed to cook until now – this book is for you. It's basic and it's simple. You can pick it up and put it down. It's not full of 'funky' this and 'pukka' that. I'm not trying to create a thousand Jamie Oliver clones or a hundred Gordon Ramsay wannabes.

This isn't a book about expensive food or fancy recipes. Instead, it's a helping hand to get you started with the basics. I'm also not telling you what to eat or what not to eat. Yes, nutrition can be a boring topic, but it's actually all about simple, good produce balanced with the nice-to-have foods. My basic recipes are easy to follow and you'll gradually learn them through practice, while my meal suggestions will be fun to cook as you gain confidence. At the same time, I'm sure that when you start to cook lovely food for yourself and your friends and family, it'll help you grow, develop and be happy.

I hope this book will kick-start your passion and enthusiasm for cooking and you will enjoy the fruits of your efforts in the kitchen.

Happy cooking!

SIMON

TO COOK OR NOT TO COOK?

COOKING OBSTACLES

OTHER PEOPLE TO CATER FOR • LACK OF SKILLS •
WORK HOURS • ALWAYS KNACKERED •
COOKING FOR ONE PERSON NOT WORTH IT • I'M ALWAYS OUT
• MONEY – CAN'T AFFORD IT • KNOWLEDGE TOO LIMITED
• COOKING IS INTIMIDATING • FANCY RECIPES PUT ME OFF
• EXPENSIVE INGREDIENTS • HAVE TO COOK FOR
DIFFERENT PEOPLE • I DON'T HAVE THE SKILLS •
MY JOB GETS IN THE WAY • I HAVE A CAREER TO
THINK ABOUT • MY COOKING KNOWLEDGE ISN'T THERE
• IT SEEMS EXPENSIVE TO BE HEALTHY •
BORING NUTRITION • TOO MUCH EFFORT •
I HATE WASHING UP • OTHER THINGS TO SPEND MONEY ON •
FAST FOOD IS CHEAPER • INGREDIENTS I DON'T RECOGNISE •
BAD HABITS ARE MY PRIORITY – SMOKING + DRINKING •
I'D RATHER GO OUT • IT'S A CHORE

COOKING INCENTIVES

LOVE CREATING NEW DISHES • FRESH IS BEST
• VIBRANT COLOURS, TEXTURES AND FLAVOURS
• CREATING NEW SKILLS FOR MYSELF • TAKES ME AWAY
FROM MY WORK • RELAXING • HAVING FRIENDS OVER •
SHARING THE COST • SPLIT THE WASHING UP •
QUICKER TO COOK FOR MYSELF • I LIKE TO BATCH COOK •
I LIKE TO COOK LIKE THE CHEFS ON TV • IT'S ACTUALLY FUN
• I CAN COOK ON A BUDGET AND SAVE MONEY •
GOOD-FOR-YOU FOOD CAN BE TASTY • BETTER VALUE •
I CAN GET EVERYONE INVOLVED • I DON'T LIKE OVER-
PRODUCED FOOD • BETTER FOR ME AND MY FAMILY
• I LOVE LEARNING THE DISHES MY GRANDMOTHER COOKED •
MY MUM'S FAVOURITES • FOOD IS PRIMAL • BETTER FOR THE
PLANET • IT'S SOCIABLE • FOOD BRINGS PEOPLE TOGETHER
• I LOVE LOCALLY PRODUCED AND NATURAL FOOD •
• NO JUNK IN THE TRUNK •
I LOVE THE SMELL OF HOMEMADE COOKING

HOW TO COOK AND KEEP COOKING

Here's a thought.

Maybe you've had a lovely childhood and have always been loved and looked after by your parents. Maybe you haven't. Either way, can you look after yourself? Be honest with yourself when answering this question.

Most people who leave school, college and/ or home to start work or go to university have to stand on their own two feet for the first time. But they can't cook for themselves. Cooking spaghetti Bolognese in a food tech class back in Year 8 may be a vague memory. It's certainly not a good enough base on which to start cooking on a daily basis. Sound familiar? Many people just can't cook with confidence in a way that will provide them with the energy and sustenance they need to survive properly.

It's easy enough to learn how to heat up ready-made meals; you just need a fork and a microwave. Then there are cooking sauces. Easy, right? Buy a packet of chicken and some rice or potatoes and add a can or jar of sauce. Hey presto – you've got a lovely meal that's been sealed up for the best part of a year, with a load of ingredients that don't belong in there just so it lasts another year. Yum! The preservation process it has gone through kills most of the vital vitamins that your body needs. So you're just eating to fill yourself up.

It's also really easy – but expensive – to purchase recipe kits. There are some good ones out there and plenty of choice – even the supermarkets are doing them now. A box or bag of goodies, a recipe card to follow and a serving suggestion. They're good, and I guess they do teach you how to cook, or rather how to heat and assemble. It's the next best thing to cooking from scratch, but it can be an expensive way to do it.

IMAGINE THIS

You understand actually how to cook. Not just that, but you enjoy the cooking process. You engage differently with your friends and family. You start to feel more energetic from eating fresh produce. Your motivation increases and you start to focus better at work, college or university. You're loving life, your relationships improve and, yes, even your work is more inviting. All because you have learned to cook.

It's powerful stuff.

COOKING FOR YOURSELF

For me, life is about living well and being happy.

It's simple really, but we can sometimes make it very complicated. Of course, some of the complications come from the fact we have to earn money to live, put a roof over our heads and buy the things we need. Quite often we forget the things that are good for us. We replace them with the things that save us time. We trick ourselves into thinking that with the time we save we can do other, more important things. Cooking is a good example of this.

Cooking is not something we should cut out of our lives. We need to eat well, and this is important for our body, our spirit and, to my mind, our soul.

Freshly cooked food is almost always better for you. Compared to convenience foods such as ready-made meals or fast food, fresh food has more vitamins and minerals, the flavours and textures are better and more natural. As a result, eating fresh food is a pleasure and you know what you're putting into your body. With convenience meals or products, you are far less likely to know the true contents of the food you are eating.

There's another reason why I think cooking is a vital part of our lives. Doing something for ourselves is a really positive and essential part of our core happiness. It seems the majority of people in the world are obsessed with television and, in particular, soaps and reality TV! They believe there's no time to cook because they are busy. But being busy watching TV is not an excuse. Many people rush home after work – all tired and hassled – to stab a ready-made meal or heat up a processed jar of sauce. They eat while watching *EastEnders, Love Island* or something similar. It seems a dreadful waste of time to me.

I challenge everyone to come home and have a conversation with a friend or loved one while cooking a meal together. Sit and talk about your day with them. This seems so much nicer, wholesome and more fulfilling. If you live on your own, I know it can be hard to cook for yourself. Trust me – it's still worth doing. Over time, you'll learn to enjoy it and appreciate it as being a good way to spend your time.

There's also the cost of convenience to think about. Supermarkets and food manufacturers all include additional costs for helping to prepare your dinner. Buying fresh food will always give you more for your money.

I recently costed a freshly cooked meal (chicken korma with rice, naan bread and poppadums) against a range of different convenience products. Firstly, I was shocked at the difference in quality. Then don't get me started on the amount of meat versus sauce. But the proof really was in the value for money that freshly cooked food provides.

HOW TO COOK FROM THIS BOOK

To help you get started, I have laid out some of the basics in cooking. It's a very simple guide. You won't need loads of equipment, but there are some basics you should have: a set of scales, a simple collection of knives, pots and pans, bowls, a chopping board, a sieve, a grater and a potato peeler. Buying from the value range in most supermarkets is a good way to stock up on cooking utensils in a cost-effective way. You can always add other items if you need them as you go along.

Always carefully read through the recipe you want to make. Cooking should not be a chore. Give yourself time to cook, see it as fun and something you will enjoy doing. Honestly, you will appreciate it once you have finished the preparation and can sit down to enjoy the fruits of your labour.

PLANNING

Once you've decided what you want to try out, make a weekly meal plan. Cooking obviously needs to fit into your schedule but try to see it as part of your day, whether it's in the evening when you get in from work or it's preparing in the morning before your shift starts. It's not that difficult to make time to write shopping lists, to prepare and cook, and, of course, to sit and enjoy a tasty, fresh meal.

SHOPPING

Create a shopping list – look at the 'Stuff you'll need' from each of my recipes. If the shop hasn't got a particular item or you can't afford it, swap it for something else. For example, instead of using a piece of cod, maybe they have pollock, which is slightly cheaper. Look for special offers and use your freezer to stock things you've bought ahead of time.

Another tip is to try going to a market at the end of the day, usually around 5.30pm. See if they'll cut you a deal – no stallholder wants to take their fresh produce back with them. Hang around and see what you can pick up.

Use supermarkets wisely. They'll try to offer you things that seem like a bargain. Very often they're not. You end up buying food you don't want and you'll end up wasting it unless you can freeze it. Only ever buy what you're sure you will make the best use of.

FOOD WASTAGE

It's possible to be creative with scraps and leftovers, so think before it's too late and you have to throw ingredients away. Keep an eye on your food stocks and try to use up food close to its use-by date. There are some great ideas for food-waste recipes on the internet, so have some fun with your old carrots, courgettes and tomatoes.

PREPARATION

Always read a recipe thoroughly. It may have a step or two to think about ahead of time. I like to prepare the vegetables and also soak or marinate things in advance. This means the cooking is much easier and you're not constantly stopping to peel or chop something.

EATING A BALANCED DIET

The reason for thinking ahead is to save time and money. Shopping for the week or at least for the next few days will mean you can take advantage of offers that do save you money. Also, spending time shopping every day seems silly to me. More importantly, by thinking ahead you will be able to give more consideration to your diet and it'll help you see if it's balanced or not.

In particular, make sure you're eating a good range of produce that incorporates all the main food groups: protein, carbohydrates, dairy, fruit, vegetables and fat. If your weekly diet is overloaded with one of these, then play with and amend your menus; drop some items and add others.

Make sure you're eating some raw vegetables, too, as this is the best way to maximise your vitamin intake. Try to think about eating at least three pieces of fruit and three types of vegetable every day. This means you'll always hit your five-a-day. It's not always possible, but if you try you might do better than you do currently. Fruit is so tasty and can satisfy a sweet tooth – we forget how lovely it is sometimes.

COOK WITH AND FOR OTHERS

Cooking with and for others is a fantastic thing. You can share the cost, the workload and, of course, the pleasure of eating. Add to this the conversation, the banter and the support you feel when engaging with others and it can be a truly powerful experience. Make sure you clean up together, too. Nobody wants to be left with all the washing up!

BULKING UP

Bulking up when cooking means you can save time on busy days. And chilling or freezing what you have cooked is a great way to make your own tasty convenience food that hasn't been splattered with preservatives. It also saves energy, and bulk-buying is very cost-effective.

When cooking for later, cool the food down to room temperature naturally and store in the refrigerator or freezer. I find labelling is useful, as it helps me to remember when the dish was cooked and what it is.

AVOID WASTE

It seems to me that we are very wasteful. I don't know why, because none of us have enough money to throw it away. So why do we throw away food?

Buying only what you need or making sure you use food up appropriately and before its use-by date is a must. Waste is bad for the environment, our pockets as well as our self-esteem, because it deflates our spirits when we waste money.

GOOD HEALTH

Good health is everyone's right. It will give you loads of energy, a healthy body, a positive outlook on life and peace of mind. These are things that don't come easily to many people – but concentrating on your health and eating well really can make the difference.

Being healthy will make you look good and feel fantastic; it'll give you clear skin, bright eyes and beautiful hair. Living as healthy a lifestyle as possible will increase your resilience to the health problems you have encountered throughout your life.

From when you're born until old age, good nutrition contributes to good health. Of course, there are other factors that have an impact on your health. Smoking, alcohol, drug abuse, your genes, the environment, pollution, accidents, mental health and other people's lack of care all play a part. Some of these you can control; others you can't. Regardless of these factors, poor nutrition can mean poor health. On the other hand, good nutrition will give you the best chance to protect your health against the elements outside your control.

Without your health, you're going nowhere fast, so it's important to take responsibility for it. Securing good health will improve your life and your chances of success.

Good health will help you defend yourself against physical and mental stress and strain and it will beef up your natural resistance to infection and disease. It will also help teens and young adults through those times of physical and mental change.

Good health and nutrition even affects the way you look. You can look your very best for life without going to a spa every day or having to visit a plastic surgeon! No pills, potions, diet sheets, expensive meal replacements or substitutes for real food are necessary. Start off by cooking a bit more than you do now. Shop for yourself and find new foods you like, while saving money on your food bill. This is where positive eating habits come from.

As time goes on, evolve your menu ideas and food choices yourself. Get your friends and family involved and share with them how you're doing. Start cooking together and enjoy shared benefits such as eating in a fun group, reducing costs and, of course, eating good, healthy food.

Don't forget to reward yourself from time to time. Good health is about balance. It's absolutely fine to indulge yourself and eat the odd treat, so long as it's part of a balanced diet.

SNAPSHOT IN HISTORY

Millions of years ago man was more like an animal, eating berries and nuts. Then something happened...

We learned to cook!

During the Stone Age, meat that had been hunted was consumed alongside milk, cereals, vegetables, roots, seeds and nuts. Although lives were short, the Stone Agers enjoyed a relatively healthy way of life.

Then the Romans came along. Their Empire spread across much of the known world at the time. Cooks used local produce wherever they travelled and discovered the glory of food using herbs and spices such as ginger, nutmeg, cinnamon, cloves, rosemary and mint. Street markets sold bread, olive oil, vegetables, fish and meat, much as our markets do today. The Roman diet was also very healthy and we can learn a lot from the way they cooked and ate.

The centuries that followed saw many changes, with wars and battles, land taken by aggressors and foods being shipped around the world, defining countries' food cultures that eventually became national dishes.

The 19th century in the UK was fairly bleak in terms of food. With massive division between classes, the rich ate well while the poor did not. Disease and illness were mostly caused by the way people ate. The rich developed liver disease, strokes, gout and heart disease, as well as obesity and alcoholism. The poor suffered from diseases and illnesses such as tuberculosis, pneumonia, scurvy and rickets, caused by malnutrition. They also developed infections and skin conditions that we now know were directly related to poor diet. Surprisingly, the food in these eras was nutritious, but not everyone could access it.

Weirdly, during World War II, despite rationing and the issues brought about by war, the nation's diet actually improved. The lack of meat and sugar in particular caused the rate of heart disease, obesity and diabetes to slow down. There's definitely a lesson to be learned in this historical fact.

A QUICK BIT OF INFO ON FOOD GROUPS

WHAT ABOUT THE FOOD GROUPS?

In the UK, the guidance we have on healthy eating is called the Eatwell Guide. Foods are divided into five different food groups and this guide shows how much of what we eat should come from each group.

All the food groups are essential and taking any one of them away will have a detrimental effect on your health. But what do they do for you and what's the current advice?

FAT

It's true that too much of the worst kind of fat leads to raised cholesterol, high blood pressure, heart disease and increased risk of certain cancers. But too little causes poor absorption of the fat-soluble vitamins A, E, D and K, which are essential for natural resistance to infection. These vitamins are also needed for healthy skin, eyes, heart and circulation, strong bones and blood clotting.

We should eat foods that are high in fat, salt and sugar less often and in small amounts. Too much of these eaten too often is a quick way to add a lot of extra energy to your diet, and unless you are very active, you're likely to gain weight. Foods that fall into this group are usually snacks such as cakes, biscuits, chocolate, crisps and savoury snacks. We don't need to eat them, and the salt and sugar (as well as energy) they contain is bad for our health if we have too much.

You'll notice that the recipes in this book tend to use olive oil. That's because the **type of fat** in olive oil (called unsaturated fat) is a healthier kind of fat. Unsaturated fats are also found in vegetable oils. These sorts of fats are better for us and they're rich sources of energy. To avoid gaining too much weight, oils should be used in small amounts.

PROTEIN

Essential for building every single one of the body's cells, protein is constantly being used and replaced. That's why it's essential for vegetarians to replace meat and fish with other good protein sources.

'Muscle builders' include beans, pulses, fish, eggs and meat. These are all great sources of protein, which builds up muscle. They also help us fight off infections and are rich in vitamins and minerals. Meat can be expensive, so choosing vegetable protein sources like pulses and beans is a great alternative. They're also lower in fat and contain more fibre, which is good for keeping our guts healthy. We should try to include at least two portions of fish a week, one of which should be an oily fish like salmon or mackerel. The fat they contain is better for our hearts than other fats. There are some great fish recipes in this book to help you. When you choose meat, select lean cuts and eat smaller amounts of red and processed meats such as bacon, ham and sausages. Many of us eat too much meat and it can add a lot of fat (especially saturated fat) to our diets. This isn't good for our hearts, while too much processed meat increases our risk of bowel cancer.

DAIRY

We should include dairy (milk, cheese, yoghurt or fromage frais) or dairy alternatives (e.g. soya) in our diets every day. These are the 'bone builders', keeping our teeth and bones strong and healthy. We get best value from these foods by choosing lower-sugar and -fat varieties where possible (e.g. semi-skimmed or skimmed milk instead of whole milk).

CARBS

Carbohydrates or starchy foods are good sources of energy. When digested, the sugars that carbohydrates contain are broken down into glucose. Glucose or blood sugar is the fuel our bodies run on. Any new glucose in our bloodstream is used up instantly and the excess is converted to glycogen and stored in the liver.

Meals should be based on potatoes, pasta, rice, bread and grains (wholegrain as much as possible). These are the 'energy boosters', full of carbohydrate energy that fuels our muscles and brains. We should have some at every meal, and to get the best value from them, we should choose wholegrain versions as much as possible (e.g. wholemeal bread and brown rice). Leaving the skins on potatoes is the easiest way to increase their nutritional value.

FRUIT & VEGETABLES

Nutrients are the fine details of what we eat and they are made up of vitamins and minerals.

Vitamins at their simplest are naturally occurring substances in foods and, without them, the body's chemistry just doesn't work. Your body needs them to work properly so you can grow and develop just like you should. When it comes to vitamins, each one has a special role to play. For example:

- **Vitamin A in carrots helps our eyesight**

- **B vitamins in whole grains help your body make energy from food**

- **Vitamin C in oranges helps our body to heal**

- **Vitamin D in milk helps our bones**

Vitamins hang out in water and fat. They can wait for up to six months in the body before they are used.

Fat-soluble vitamins are stored in the fat tissues and in the liver, waiting until they are needed.

Water-soluble vitamins are different. When you eat foods that contain these vitamins, the vitamins travel around the body in your bloodstream and whatever your body doesn't use, it comes out in your urine.

Vitamin A – Plays an important part in healthy eyesight, it's great for night vision and seeing colours. It can also help fight infection by boosting our immune system. Milk, liver, orange fruits and vegetables like carrots, cantaloupe melons and sweet potatoes, and dark leafy green vegetables such as kale, collards and spinach.

B Vitamins – There's more than one B vitamin. Here's the list: B1, B2, B6, B12, niacin, folic acid, biotin and pantothenic acid. B vitamins are good for making energy and help to release it in the body. This group of vitamins is also involved in making red blood cells, which carry oxygen around the body. Every part of the body needs oxygen, so these vitamins are really important. Whole grains, such as wheat and oats, also fish and seafood. Poultry and meats, eggs, dairy such as milk and yoghurt. Leafy vegetables and peas and beans.

Vitamin C – This vitamin is important for keeping body tissues such as gums, bones and blood vessels in good shape. It is also important to help heal a cut or wound and helps the body fight infection. Citrus fruit, strawberries, tomatoes, broccoli, cabbage, kiwi fruit and red peppers.

Vitamin D – For healthy bones and strong teeth you need vitamin D. It helps the body absorb the amount of calcium it needs. Vitamin D is made in the skin when exposed to the sunlight, or you can get it from food. Milk fortified with vitamin D, fish, egg yolks, liver and fortified cereals.

Vitamin E – Everybody needs vitamin E. This vitamin protects your cells and tissues from damage. It is also important for the health of our red blood cells. Whole grains, wheatgerm, leafy vegetables, vegetable oils such as sunflower, rapeseed or canola and olive. Egg yolks, nuts and seeds.

Vitamin K – This vitamin is the clot master! Remember when you cut yourself, your blood clots. This occurs when certain cells in your blood stick and glue together on the surface to help stop the bleeding. Leafy vegetables, dairy products such as milk and yoghurt, broccoli and soya bean oil.

EAT AT LEAST 5 portions of fruit and vegetables a day. This can include fresh, frozen, canned, dried and juiced fruits and vegetables. However, only drink a maximum of 150ml/ ⅔ cup juices and smoothies, as they contain a lot of sugar in liquid form. Most of us don't

eat enough fruit and vegetables, yet they are filling, great for keeping our guts working and contain energy in a form we can use easily. That's why athletes eat bananas to keep them going!

Minerals – These are the other essential group of nutrients; we need some of them more than others. They help our to bodies to grow, develop and stay healthy. The body uses minerals to perform many different functions from building strong bones to transforming nerve impulses. Some minerals are even used to make hormones or maintain a normal heartbeat.

Calcium – This is a top mineral when it comes to your bones and teeth. Found in dairy such as milk, cheese and yoghurt.

Iron – It helps in the formation of haemoglobin, which is the part of the red blood cells that carries oxygen from your lungs to the rest of your body. Red meat, tuna, salmon, eggs, beans, leafy vegetables like broccoli and whole grains like wheat or oats.

Potassium – Keeps your muscles and nervous system working properly. Bananas, tomatoes, potatoes, green leaves like spinach, citrus fruit such as oranges, and legumes like green beans, split peas and lentils.

Zinc – This helps your immune system, which is your body's system for fighting off illness and infections. It also promotes cell growth and helps heal wounds, such as cuts. Beef, pork, nuts such as cashews, almonds and peanuts, and also legumes like green beans, split peas and lentils.

When people don't get enough of these important minerals, they can have health problems. For example, not enough calcium can lead to weaker bones, especially in children and the elderly.

IT'S ALSO IMPORTANT TO NOTE:

We need to drink plenty of fluids. The general advice is that we need six to eight glasses of fluids a day, but many of us may need even more, especially when we're active or in hot weather. Water, low-fat milks and low sugar or sugar-free drinks like tea and coffee all count. Sugary drinks, whether they're still or sparkling, should be chosen only occasionally. For many of us they add a lot of extra calories (energy) and sugar to our diets, which is bad news for our waistlines and our teeth.

There is a special group of nutrients called phytochemicals that include some vitamins and some minerals. A host of other natural plant chemicals – known as antioxidants – have a powerful, protective quality, fighting off the damaging effects of free radicals that are naturally produced by our bodies.

Phytochemicals are found in fruits, vegetables, grains, beans and other plants. Some of these phytochemicals are believed to protect cells from damage that could lead to cancers. Research shows that some phytochemicals may:

- Help stop the formation of potential cancer-causing substances (carcinogens)
- Help stop carcinogens from attacking cells
- Help cells wipe out any cancer-like changes

Some of the most beneficial phytochemicals are:

- Beta carotene, found in orange-coloured fruits and vegetables such as carrots
- Resveratrol in red wine
- Polyphenols in tea
- Isothiocyanates in the cabbage family, such as bok choy, spring greens, broccoli,

Brussels sprouts, kohlrabi, kale, mustard greens, turnip greens and cauliflower

FOOD SUPPLEMENTS

There is no evidence that taking vitamin, mineral or phytochemical supplements is as good for us as eating whole fruit, vegetables, beans and grains that contain them. Most experts would say a balanced diet that contains a good mixture is best for our bodies. Loading up on one or more in a pill form probably won't be as beneficial as eating five or more portions of fruit and vegetables.

READING FOOD LABELS

What we eat is vital for our health and wellbeing, so information is provided on food labels to help us make healthier choices. In the UK we use traffic light labelling. The colours red, amber and green tell us if the food contains high, medium or low levels of fat, saturated fat, sugar and salt. Red means high, amber means medium and green means low. So when more green is seen on the label, the food is healthier. Amber means the food is neither high nor low, so it is fine to eat those foods most of the time. Red on the label means we should choose those foods less often and eat them in smaller quantities when we do choose them.

EAT SPARINGLY

EAT IN MODERATION

EAT PLENTY

There's a lot of information out there about different food groups, about what's good and bad for us and how much you should eat. I encourage you to read even more about these groups along your journey. The NHS Live Well website (www.nhs.uk/LiveWell) is a great place to start for the most up-to-date advice.

10 BITS OF ADVICE FROM ME

If you take just 10 messages away from this book, these are the pieces of advice I think are more important than anything else.

1. Eat a mixed diet, trying to eat as many different kinds of foods as possible.

2. Try to eat regular meals and make time really to enjoy and digest them.

3. Eat loads of fresh fruit, salads and vegetables – the green, leafy ones are particularly good for you.

4. They may seem boring but try to develop a taste for wholegrain cereals and breads.

5. Make sure you're getting most of your protein from fish, poultry, pulses and less from red meat, which should be lean when you do eat it.

6. Eat eggs, cheese and other dairy products, but don't eat too much at a time.

7. Use plenty of seeds, unsalted nuts and dried fruit, adding them to your meals and using them as nourishing snacks.

8. Drink loads of water, some fresh fruit and vegetable juices and only small quantities of coffee, tea and booze.

9. Bread, pasta, rice and potatoes are very healthy. Have plenty but watch what you do with them. Lashings of butter, creamy sauces and chips are not good for you.

10. Make sure that at least one-third of your daily food starts out as fresh, raw produce. The other two-thirds should come from your kitchen. There's nothing more wholesome and nourishing than home-cooked food. It's also a lot cheaper and you get more for your money than from takeaways, frozen, canned or ready-made meals.

Bonus bit of advice
There's no need to feel you can't have a treat. As long as you're sticking to the spirit of this book, you don't need to become some foodie freak. Just try to let chocolate, salty snacks and burgers be a treat rather than part of your staple diet.

GOING FROM TEENS TO YOUNG ADULTHOOD

You have already started growing up. You're now independent and may be starting your first job, or you're setting off for college or university. This is a time when there is a lot of growth, development and hormonal change going on inside you, so you need the best possible nutrition. One thing is for sure – you need plenty of energy to be able to cope with moving yourself on to a new chapter in life.

KEEP MOVING!

Don't become a couch potato. Sometimes this is easily done when starting a different routine or living somewhere new. Exercise not only has physical benefits, but the endorphins released by the brain contribute to a feel-good factor that has a positive influence on your mood. Take up a sport or simply go for brisk walks. Whatever you do, include some form of movement or activity in your life.

THREE MEALS A DAY ARE ESSENTIAL

I know you've heard it before, but breakfast is really important. You can't drive a car without petrol. It's the same with your body. Muesli or porridge is perfect for long, slow energy release that will keep you fuelled up for hours. Top it with fresh fruit and you won't need a snack before lunchtime.

Lunch is as important and sandwiches are simple to make – ensure you use wholemeal bread. Cheese, tuna, sardines or chicken are good fillings for protein. Add parsley, baby spinach or cress – they have high nutritional value and are great for the skin. Vegetable sticks and fresh fruit are great accompaniments to round off lunch.

For dinner, try to sit down for the occasion and invite friends over to share the cost of cooking and eating together. Include lots of vegetables and salads in your evening meals. Try to eat at least one raw vegetable each night – you'll soon start to notice a difference. One of the easiest ways to do this is to eat a side salad.

EATING AT HOME

When you live on your own, cooking can be a chore or become unimportant. Feeling like this can lead to you making poor choices for snacks and selecting takeaways or ready-made meals. Prepare a ready-to-eat vegetable box, have a bowl of fruit on the side to dip into and make sure your cupboard has tins of tuna, salmon, sardines, tomatoes and kidney beans. Brown rice, pasta and good-quality pasta sauces are also good staples to have close at hand. This will make it easier for you to make better choices when you're feeling less motivated to cook.

EATING AT WORK OR COLLEGE

Remember cooking should be a pleasure, even if you are on your own. You're worth the effort and you will enjoy what you cook. Try new things and invite friends or neighbours round. Stockpile and freeze to make cooking better for your wallet and a go-to option instead of using more convenient but less nutritious alternatives.

IT'S NEVER BEEN A BETTER TIME TO START FEEDING YOUR BRAIN

Most canteens, supermarkets and sandwich bars sell ready-to-eat salads but at inflated prices. Make them at home for a quarter of the price and include ingredients such as carrots, coleslaw, apples, celery, nuts and brown rice. Add a glass of milk or a carton of yoghurt, as well as a piece of fruit, and you'll be ready for an afternoon of work.

The key to your personal success, no matter what has happened to you in the past, is to start using your brain. You may need to sit exams, pass tests, train for a new job or get coursework done. If you don't feed your brain with the right food, it can have a detrimental effect on its performance.

The brain needs a constant supply of sugar and oxygen to do its job properly. If the brain

doesn't get a proper supply of them, you can guarantee poor performance and worse memory and concentration. You may also suffer mood swings, irritability, bad temper and headaches. To solve this problem, eat at least every three hours, particularly if you're taking exams or working hard on a problem-solving exercise.

Eating foods that are nutrient-rich is vital, as they give you an adequate and constant supply of vitamins A and B, as well as iron, zinc, fatty acids and carotenoids. This may seem like a foreign language to you, but it's really easy. Just make sure you eat shellfish, oily fish, meat and poultry, wholegrain cereals, nuts and seeds, fresh fruit, vegetables and salads – particularly dark green, red and orange coloured fruit and vegetables. You'll be feeling better in no time.

HOW CAN FOOD HELP ME?

Obesity – If you're overweight and trying to lose some of it, don't cut down on food that helps you grow and provides you with energy.

Being overweight has a long-term detrimental effect on your body that can lead you to diabetes, joint problems, high blood pressure, high cholesterol and risk of heart disease. It can also have a social consequence. Being overweight carries an emotional burden and can lead to psychological disturbance, relationship problems, lack of self-esteem, poor self-image and can limit your enjoyment of life. It can also restrict your exercise opportunities.

The main factors involved in being overweight are excess fat and sugar in your diet. Many processed and takeaway foods contain fats that are unhealthy and unsaturated, but they also have hidden amounts of sugar. If you have a sweet tooth, go for bananas, apples or semi-dried fruit instead, as these give you an instant energy lift.

Try to eat lots of good carbohydrates, fresh fruit and vegetables, remove all fat from meat and eat plenty of fresh fish and poultry. Choose semi-skimmed or skimmed milk and look for lower-fat cheese and yoghurts. Avoid thickened and creamy sauces and watch out for hidden fats and sugars. Cut right back on alcohol. Eat nourishing cereals and plenty of wholemeal bread with hardly any spread but, most importantly, never miss breakfast. Grill or steam your food – don't fry it. Lastly, try to use a smaller plate to help control portion sizes and present your food nicely on it. Don't eat in front of the TV, take your time eating it and you'll feel satisfied with what you've eaten.

ANOREXIA

Commonly thought of as being something that affects females, anorexia is a condition that actually affects anyone. As well as support from professionals, a vital mineral can help combat anorexia. A lack of zinc destroys the taste buds and zaps the appetite. Zinc can therefore help to bring back the enjoyment of food – good sources include prawns, liver, lean meat, wheat germ, sesame and pumpkin seeds, mackerel, cheese and green vegetables.

STRESS

We all have stress, some more than others for many different reasons. Try to eat food regularly and have food that is rich in B vitamins such as wholegrain cereals, liver, meat, fish and green, leafy vegetables. Try not to drink too much coffee or try it decaffeinated. Orange juice is a good alternative, as it has plenty of vitamin C.

LOW ENERGY

Young people, and girls in particular, need to watch their iron reserves. Make sure you stock up on foods that are rich in iron such as spinach, egg yolks, lentils, nuts, seeds, raisins, dates and liver. Drinking tea and coffee while eating the above can hinder the body's absorption of iron, but vitamin C has the opposite effect, so eating fruit, a salad or drinking orange juice is a great idea.

SKIN PROBLEMS

If you're watching your fat and sugar intake, skin problems should take care of themselves. Eating wholegrain cereals are great for zinc, which is good for the skin. Your best friend should be green, leafy foods such as cabbage, as it's full of beta carotene. Your body turns this into vitamin

A – vital for healthy skin and clear eyes. Green also means it contains chlorophyll, which has a cleansing, nourishing and antibacterial effect on the skin. A spoonful of parsley each day is fabulous for your complexion.

MENSTRUAL PROBLEMS

These can be a real drag: cramps, irritability, tension, nausea and bloating can be a monthly trial. Food can come to the rescue once again. Wholegrain cereals, nuts and seeds (particularly almonds), oats, sesame and sunflower seeds have loads of vitamins and nutrients that will help. Bananas are also a wonderful food rich in iron and potassium, which will help your kidneys cope with water-retention problems. They're filling and nourishing, too, with only around 90 calories.

SMOKING AND DRINKING

If you have taken on these habits you need to quickly understand that they are both expensive and very bad for your health. I've heard many excuses as to why people smoke and continue to do so. Drinkers tell me their excess drinking is just about having fun.

Our bodies are not made to cope with these excesses. The liver has a low resistance to alcohol, while smoking and drinking generates free radical activity that cause dangerous chemicals to damage our body's cells. This increases the rate of heart disease, cancer and also wrinkles.

I know it sounds lame, but I'm sure cigarettes are about boredom. Replace them with sunflower seeds, which are great to nibble on and are little powerhouses of good nutrition.

Don't be dragged into the binge-drinking culture around you either. You're cleverer than that. The older you get, the harder it is to take yourself away from those habits and the longer it takes to recover.

DRUGS

Well, what can I say? Drugs form a slippery slope that will take you to many dark places. It's best to steer clear or get off them as fast as you can. I don't know of any food that can bring people back from the dead.

TOP FOODS FOR TOP PEOPLE

Almonds

A concentrated food rich in protein and good fats, zinc, magnesium, potassium and iron as well as calcium and B vitamins.

Apricots

Fantastic for instant energy release from their natural sugars, and beta carotene.

Avocados

Very nutritious and filling but high in calories, so be careful!

Bananas

High in potassium, great for hearts and full of fibre.

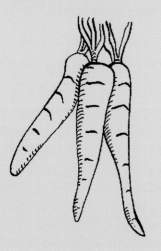

Beans

All beans are great, from baked to borlotti. They're good sources of energy, protein and fibre.

Beef

Good source of protein, B vitamins and minerals. Be aware of fat, particularly in mince (always check the content percentage) – it's very often added to bulk it out.

Beetroot

Helps improve the oxygen-carrying capacity of blood.

Blueberries

These are particularly healthy as they have a very high antioxidant capacity, so they're able to help protect the body from cancer and age-related diseases. They promote healthy skin, eyes and brain.

Broccoli

Rich in vitamins A and C. It also provides iron, calcium and potassium, and folic acid. No wonder it's a superfood.

Carrots

A single carrot can supply enough vitamin A for the whole day.

Cauliflower

Great for strong bones, healthy hair and firm skin.

Celery

Great nerve tonic and can be eaten as a remedy for fluid retention during a period.

Cereals

The name given to the seeds of a group of plants from the grass family. The most important cereals grown in the world are barley, maize, millet, oats, rice, rye and wheat. Their nutritional value is much the same and their main constituents are energy-providing starches.

Cheese

Rich in protein and calcium as well B vitamins, vitamins A, D and E. Feta, Edam, cottage and curd cheeses are low in fat.

Dairy foods

Foods such as milk, yoghurt and cheese are valuable sources of essential nutrients, especially during pregnancy, breastfeeding and for your children. Milk is a cheap and easily consumed, rich source of calcium.

Dates

Great to satisfy a sweet tooth, dates are a supply of badly needed iron. They're also high in potassium.

Eggs

These are the original low-calorie convenience food. They are a good source of protein, supplying around 6g a time.

Fish

Many home cooks are afraid of fish. They haven't grown up seeing their mothers buy and prepare it, so they don't know what to do with it unless it comes pre-packed and ready to heat. Fish is an exceptional source of protein and minerals; sea fish is particularly valuable for its high iodine content. Oily fish is high in vitamins A, D and E as well as omega 3 – great for boosting your brain and good for your heart.

Flaxseed oil

Must be non-GM and preferably organic. A rich source in essential fatty acids for the brain, central nervous function and hormone regulation.

Fruit

Provides essential vitamins, minerals and natural phytochemicals. Those who live longer and free of strokes, high blood pressure and heart disease have enjoyed a high consumption of fruit throughout their lives.

Grapes

Easy to digest, grapes are uniquely nourishing and fortifying.

Green vegetables

Cabbage, brussels sprouts and spinach are great for skin protection and anticancer properties. They're also rammed full of vitamin K, essential for blood clotting. (Young babies can't eat green veg.)

Kiwi fruit

With twice the vitamin C of an orange, more fibre than an apple, as much vitamin E as an avocado and lots of potassium, kiwis are great for fatigue and poor digestion.

Lentils

These are rich in protein, iron and zinc.

Liver

Rich in iron and B vitamins.

Meat and poultry

Whether beef, lamb, poultry or game, they are extremely nutritious. These foods are excellent sources of protein, rich providers of the most easily absorbed iron and effective providers of B vitamins and other minerals. Always remove excess fat when possible.

Melon

The cantaloupe and Ogen varieties are rich in vitamin A.

Oats and wholegrain cereals

Boring I know, but excellent for energy that slowly releases throughout the day.

Oily fish (fresh, smoked or tinned)

With the exception of tinned tuna, oily fish is rich in essential fatty acids (omega 3 and 6) of which the brain needs loads.

Oranges

Eating a whole orange before a meal helps absorb iron, calcium and other useful minerals from food. And they're great for vitamin C, of course.

Parsley

Rich in vitamins A and C, as well as iron.

Porridge and oatmeal

These make a fantastic start to any day.

Potatoes

These are good news for the intelligent slimmer. Even a whopping baked potato, crispy skin and all, is only 200 calories.

Pulses

Whether you're eating baked beans or an Indian dahl, pulses are one of the most ancient of our staple foods. Eating them provides abundant benefits, including protein and vitamins. They're also very filling and cheap!

Pumpkin seeds

They make a great snack providing valuable B vitamins, iron, zinc and unsaturated fatty acids.

Rosemary

Ideal for essential oils that stimulate brain function and improve memory and concentration.

Sage

A powerful healing and antiseptic herb.

Sardines

These are every woman's friend, rich in protein, vitamins D and B12, calcium and easy-to-absorb iron and zinc. Of course, omega 3 is a brain booster too and brilliant for the heart.

Seeds and nuts

Good for brain nutrition and great for keeping hunger at bay, seeds and nuts also lift up salads and crumbles. Try to keep away from salted and roasted varieties, as they're bad for the heart and increase blood pressure.

Shellfish

Essential for zinc, protein and some essential fatty acids. Great for the brain!

Spinach

This owes its deep dark green colour to chlorophyll. It's a superfood that really packs a powerful punch for the brain and for optimum blood pressure.

Sprouting beans

These beans are weight for weight among the richest food sources for brain nutrients.

Sprouting seeds

The most live and nutritious food that can grow on your windowsill.

Strawberries

The only fruit with seeds on the outside are low in fat and calories. They're also high in vitamin C, fibre, folic acid and potassium, and they can reduce the risk of cancer and heart attacks.

Sunflower seeds

Packed full of unsaturated fats and protein and generally wonderful nutrition.

Thyme

Has powerful antiviral and antibacterial properties.

Tuna

Fresh tuna contains omega 3 – good fats that have a protective action on the heart – but tinned tuna is a poor source of these oils. Tinned salmon, sardines, mackerel and pilchards are better sources.

Vegetables

In the UK and USA, we have developed a meat and two veg culture. Actually, in most countries their intake of fresh vegetables is much higher and in general their people's life expectancy is higher.

Walnuts

High in protein, B vitamins, calcium, potassium, phosphorus, zinc and essential fatty acids. Another superfood and a great all-rounder.

COOKING

I've always loved cooking. To me, there's nothing better than getting into the kitchen with some fresh produce and preparing a meal for my friends, family or just for myself.

It's a gift not a chore. As long as you see it that way, it's always a pleasure.

The recipes in this book are ideal for getting stuck into while developing your cooking skills. They won't cost the earth and you may well be able to stock up on them for the week. You could even freeze portions for the future – your very own ready-made meals, although you'll know they're made of fresh, wholesome ingredients.

Take time to shop for the best-quality ingredients you can afford. Once you're in the kitchen and cooking, take your time to get really great results and don't start cooking a recipe you don't have time for. Food should taste good. Once you know these recipes, you can start to adapt them as you wish to and add some of your own personality to them. Sit down to eat and enjoy your efforts. Share with others. It'll give you some feel-good factor to spend time with friends and family, watching how they appreciate the food too. Get them to help clear away to thank you for your efforts – nobody likes clearing up, after all!

PUTTING THE KIT IN THE KITCHEN

A safe working area is essential, whether you're a professional or a home cook. Nobody should become ill from eating food. Using the right equipment is also essential; it makes life easier and helps cooking to be a pleasure and not a chore. It's important to respect your kitchen equipment and tidy up when you're finished. As well as being annoying for other people you may share a kitchen with, not cleaning up straight afterwards shortens the lifespan of kitchen equipment.

Healthy chopping boards
Buy coloured chopping boards to distinguish them from each other. Have a minimum of two to three different kinds and keep them for different jobs when cooking. The following colours are what professional chefs use:

- Red – raw meat
- Yellow – cooked meat and fish
- Blue – fish
- Brown – salad and vegetables
- White – dairy

Good pans
Get stainless-steel pans if you can. There's no need to buy non-stick ones, except for a frying pan.

A wok is handy for stir-fries and is good for fast cooking.

Selection of hand tools
Wooden or plastic spoons, measuring spoons, a whisk, cheese grater, potato peeler and lemon juicer are all basic utensils necessary for cooking.

Potato ricer
This is the best tool to make mashed potato and it can be used for other root vegetables too.

Selection of plastic bowls

In my view, having a good selection of bowls to keep prepared ingredients in is essential. It means you can be organised, which helps make cooking a pleasure.

Large mixing bowls

These are perfect for making bread and tossing salads, and ideal for punch at parties.

Hand blender

A hand blender is great for smoothies, fresh soups, salad dressings and batters.

Some 'nice to haves'

A proper juicer is great to get the very maximum out of your fruit and vegetables. A liquidiser or bar blender is ideal for making fresh soup and smoothies. In my opinion, a good-quality food processor is not a luxury. It's really useful for chopping, mixing, crushing, grinding and beating any ingredient in seconds.

TOP FOOD STORAGE TIPS

- Always wash your hands before cooking and immediately after handling food, or more frequently as required.
- Always keep cooked meat separate from fresh, raw meat. In the fridge, store raw meat at the very bottom so no blood can drip onto other food.
- Use separate chopping boards for meat, vegetables and fish.
- Keep raw food off the cooked food chopping boards.
- Keep vegetables in a cool place with plenty of airflow.
- Salad stuff should be kept in a separate drawer in the fridge.
- If you use half a tin of something, put the remainder in a covered plastic container and keep it in the fridge. Don't leave it in the tin.
- Remember to label food once it's out of the original packaging so you remember how old it is.

KNIVES

Knives are essential when cooking. You don't need loads of different ones, but sharpness is important. Knives are an investment and there are many different qualities to look for. Buy what you can afford now and, as you become more experienced and increasingly value your time in the kitchen, you can add to your collection. Here's a simple guide about what to buy and how to keep them sharp.

USING KNIVES

Be careful when using knives; they're sharp and can hurt you or others if you don't concentrate. Hold the knife firmly by grasping it with your fingers around the handle. Don't allow your fingers to touch the blade as you grip the handle.

Don't walk around with a knife pointing up – point it down at all times.
Never run around and muck about, and always put a knife down when you're talking. Hand it over by the handle if you need to pass it to someone. Keep the sharp edge away from you when you clean it. Don't complicate your chopping board; take non-essential items off the board, especially other knives.

Keep knives visible
Hiding knives under clothes is dangerous, as is carrying them on top of boards or containers, as they can fall off and cut someone.

Keep your knives clean and grease-free
Damaged knives can be dangerous, so replace them if necessary. Wash them each and every time you use them, especially after tasks such as cutting raw meat and fish.

Don't forget that a knife is a chef's most important piece of equipment. Look after your knives and they will get the job done. Don't and you won't!

ESSENTIAL KNIVES TO HAVE IN YOUR KITCHEN

Chopping knife: A broad-bladed knife that can chop, slice, cut and shred vegetables, meat and fruit.

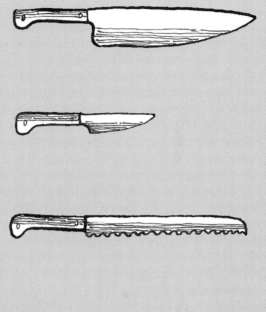

Paring knife: A small multi-purpose knife that is used to top and tail, peel and cut small vegetables and fruit.

Serrated knife: A knife used for cutting bread, pastry and tomatoes. It has sharp teeth and should be used with caution.

Steel: Used for sharpening knives. It's a great tool, but used in the wrong way it can be dangerous.

Non-essential knives but nice to have

Filleting knife: It has a flexible blade and allows you to fillet fish without being too heavy-handed.

Boning knife: A short-bladed knife that does not flex. Used for taking meat off the bone.

KEEP IT SAFE WHILE YOU EAT
SAFETY AND HYGIENE

Without going into too much detail, it's obviously important to prepare and cook in a safe and hygienic environment. So here are some pointers to think about when cooking at home.

PERSONAL HYGIENE

Wash your hands with hot water and soap before, during and after each task you do. This way you know you're not spreading bacteria around your kitchen surfaces or equipment. Do not cook food for others if you have been feeling sick or had diarrhoea, unless you have been free of the symptoms for 24 hours. Cooking for yourself is ok.

CUTS AND BURNS

All cuts and burns must be covered and kept away from food. Protect yourself by wearing an apron to avoid spills that can burn or mess up your clothes. Use an oven cloth or glove to make sure you avoid getting burned. Using sharp knives give more precision so tend to avoid cuts and also cause less damage if you do cut yourself. Keep a first-aid kit handy to make sure you can quickly take care of any injuries. Clean any burn or cut under cold water, dry it thoroughly and apply a waterproof plaster. If any cut continues to bleed and is not contained by the dressing, seek help. Burns need light, sterile dressings and sometimes need medical attention.

FOOD SAFETY

No food should ever harm the person eating it, so preparing and cooking in a safe manner is fundamental. Taking responsibility for the way it is managed is hugely important, especially when cooking for babies, older people, pregnant women and those who may not be well. Food poisoning is a digestive illness caused by food that is contaminated with bacteria and their toxins. Symptoms can include nausea, vomiting, diarrhoea, stomach pain and dehydration.

HIGH-RISK FOODS

Although care should be taken when you are cooking all foods, extra care is needed when cooking high-risk food such as soups, stocks and sauces, egg dishes, milk and cheese products and, of course, meat and fish. You need to ensure these are cooked through and have reached a certain temperature before they're safe to eat. If you have leftovers, cool the food quickly to prevent harmful bacteria from forming and then store in the fridge. Be especially careful with rice, and try to cool and store it within an hour. Also take care when reheating food; making sure it's hot is vital.

FOOD STORAGE

Once you have brought your shopping home, store it correctly, making sure chilled food goes in the fridge and ensure the temperature of the fridge never goes higher than 5°C/41°F. Frozen food should be stored at -18°C/-0.4°F and must be thoroughly thawed out before cooking, unless the manufacturers state it can be cooked from frozen.

All raw meat and fish should be covered adequately and stored at the bottom of the fridge to avoid it dripping onto ready-to-eat food. All dairy and egg products should be stored in the fridge, as well as some fruit, vegetables and salads.

Dry ingredients will be fine at room temperature and stored in a cupboard.

KITCHEN CLEANING

Make sure your kitchen is clean and tidy at all times. After cooking, spend a few minutes washing the surfaces, the equipment used and put everything away. Using a food-safe sanitiser is highly recommended.

10 WAYS TO PREVENT FOOD POISONING

1. WASH YOUR HANDS WITH HOT SOAPY WATER, ESPECIALLY AFTER GOING TO THE TOILET, BLOWING YOUR NOSE AND TOUCHING ANIMALS.

2. WASH KITCHEN WORKTOPS BEFORE, DURING AND AFTER PREPARING FOOD, PARTICULARLY WHEN USING RAW MEAT, FISH, EGGS AND VEGETABLES.

3. WASH DISHCLOTHS AND TEA TOWELS REGULARLY, AS THESE ARE THE PERFECT PLACES IN WHICH GERMS CAN GROW AND SPREAD.

4. USE SEPARATE CHOPPING BOARDS FOR READY-TO-EAT FOOD AND RAW FOOD.

5. KEEP RAW MEAT SEPARATE FROM OTHER FOOD WHEN SHOPPING AND WHEN PUTTING YOUR SHOPPING IN BAGS. KEEP RAW MEAT IN THE BOTTOM OF THE FRIDGE SO IT CAN'T DRIP ONTO OTHER FOOD.

6. COOK FOOD THOROUGHLY, ESPECIALLY POULTRY AND KEBABS. CHECK THERE IS NO PINK MEAT INSIDE BEFORE EATING.

7. DON'T WASH RAW MEAT, ESPECIALLY CHICKEN, AS THIS CAN SPREAD BACTERIA AROUND THE KITCHEN. I PERSONALLY NEVER FREEZE CHICKEN FOR THIS REASON.

8. KEEP THE FRIDGE BELOW 5°C/41°F AND DON'T OVERSTUFF THE FRIDGE, TO ENSURE THE TEMPERATURE REMAINS CONSTANT.

9. COOL LEFTOVERS QUICKLY AND NEVER PUT LEFTOVER FOOD IN THE FRIDGE WHILE IT IS STILL WARM OR HOT.

10. RESPECT ALL USE-BY DATES ON THE FOOD YOU BUY AND USE LEFTOVERS WITHIN TWO DAYS.

COOKING METHODS

I've given a lot of thought to which cooking methods to include here, and I'd suggest giving them all a try. Some might fit your style more than others, but you'll never know unless you give them a shot.

BOILING

This means immersing food in rapidly boiling water (100°C/212°F), then reducing it to a simmer. It's a healthy way to cook, as there's no fat involved. If done in the right way, you will retain most of the vitamins in the food. Overboiling means boiling something for too long, which can boil away the goodness and break down the textures. The food will not taste very nice either. So watch what you cook and pay attention to cooking times.

POACHING

This means cooking something at just under boiling point. This is far gentler than boiling, and care needs to be taken as poaching tends to involve softer, trickier ingredients. Eggs are poached in water, and fish and poultry can be poached in stock for a delicate and healthy way to prepare food.

STEAMING

This is cooking under the pressure of steam from boiling water. At home it's a bit more difficult to steam. You can try by boiling a little water in a pan, place a colander or tray with holes over the top and cover with a lid. It's a quick and brilliant way to cook, as food tends to retain much more of its goodness. Fish, vegetables and poultry are at their best and healthiest when steamed.

STEWING

This is a lovely way to cook. The food is completely covered by the cooking liquid and both are served together. Some stews are cooked on top of the stove and some in the oven; we tend to call them casseroles. Dice the meat, fish and/or vegetables into chunks, seal off and dust with flour, add cooking liquid and simmer until thickened and cooked through.

BRAISING

Braising is similar to stewing, but uses larger pieces of beef, chicken and game, which can be cooked in the oven or on top of the stove. Braising food uses less liquid than stewing so frequent basting is necessary. When ready, the food is robust with lots of flavour.

BAKING

This is when the water in food creates steam and, along with the heat from the oven, the food gets cooked. You can bake most food, but this method tends to be mostly used for cakes, bread and jacket potatoes, as well as egg custards, which need gentle baking.

ROASTING

Roasting is cooking in a dry heat with added fat or oil. It can be done on a spit but is generally done in the oven. You can roast most food, including meat joints, poultry, fish and vegetables.

GRILLING

Grilling is a fast method of cookery. You can get top-down or bottom-up heat grills. Both work with radiant heat. Char-grills use iron bars that sear the food.

FRYING

This means preheating fat or oil to cook food. Shallow-frying is usually done in a frying pan and uses minimal amounts of fat or oil, whereas deep-frying is often done in a special fryer and uses a lot more fat. The food is submerged in hot oil until it is cooked through and golden brown. Cooking with both methods produces a colouring process that is extremely tasty. However, it's not seen as the healthiest method of cookery and shouldn't be used too often. It can also be very dangerous, so great care should be taken when deep-frying.

STIR-FRYING

In this case, food is fast-fried in a wok, using a minimal amount of oil. It's deemed a healthier option to shallow-frying.

MICROWAVING

Microwaves are very handy, but I personally prefer using the more traditional cooking methods. The microwave uses the same waves that carry TV signals. That doesn't sound like a very 'foodie' way to cook, so I tend to only use it when needs must. Microwaves can be handy for heating up or defrosting non high-risk foods such as soups and bread.

PRACTICAL KITCHEN TIPS

I always try to follow these tips to ensure cooking runs smoothly.

Taking time for cooking really helps; being rushed will only make you feel stressed and you won't enjoy it.

Cooking is messy, but clearing and cleaning as you go makes it light work at the end. Then you can relax and enjoy what you've made.

Think ahead and plan what you want to do – researching and reading your recipes thoroughly will make the execution more successful.

Read through your recipe before starting. This is important to make sure you understand the order of preparation and cooking, so there are no surprises along the way.

Get all your equipment and ingredients ready before you start. This means you won't be running around trying to find things while you're cooking.

Always think about food safety. Keep raw meat and fish away from ready-to-eat foods, clean and sanitise regularly after each job, and wash your hands before and after each and every task.

Taste as you go. You can correct seasoning and add a flavour if it's lacking. But most of all, it ensures you're on top of your ingredients. By tasting, you will know if something's missing.

Try new processes and techniques. This makes meals more interesting and helps you to build skills. Don't worry if you make mistakes; it's all part of learning.

Make it fun. Invite friends to help share the cooking, cleaning and, of course, the eating. It makes it all worthwhile.

BORING STUFF THAT MAKES SENSE

Before we get to the recipes, a note about keeping things simple and organised. They might be things you've heard already from a parent or a teacher, and they probably make total sense.

The better your ingredients and the simpler the cooking process, the healthier it will be for you. It'll probably be a lot tastier than over-prepared food too.

Most of the dishes coming up are relatively simple to prepare, but I would suggest you read through the recipe first. It's much better to understand all the ingredients and stages before commencing.

Generally, I like to prepare all my ingredients before cooking. This means I can concentrate on the cooking fully. It helps ensure I don't miss something, or even burn it while doing something else.

Think about the week ahead. If you're having roast chicken, buy a whole chicken. It may be a little more expensive, but you'll probably have enough left over for a stir-fry the next day. You can make soup with the carcass too. This is called 'chain cooking' and can save you a lot of money.

Make sure all your food is in date, and that all your eggs are certified and stamped with the British Lion. This ensures they're salmonella-free, which is especially important when cooking for young children and elderly people.

When preparing some recipes, see if you can prepare enough for the week, for example, muesli or vinaigrette. Both of these can be made in advance and kept for several days easily saving you time and money, not to mention washing up.

If you're making spaghetti Bolognese, for example, make enough sauce for two or three meals. You could freeze some in small sealable bags or tubs. Make sure it's at room temperature and labelled before storing in the freezer!

Reference Intakes

You'll see 'reference intakes' referred to on food labels. They show you the maximum amount of calories and nutrients you should eat in a day.

Daily reference intakes for adults are:

Energy: 8,400kJ/2,000kcal

Total fat: less than 70g

Saturates: less than 20g

Carbohydrates: at least 260g

Total sugars: 90g

Protein: 50g

Salt: less than 6g

The reference intake for total sugars includes sugars from milk and fruit, as well as added sugar.

Reference intakes aren't meant to be targets. They just give you a rough idea of how much energy you should be eating each day, and how much fat, sugar, salt and so on.

Unless the label says otherwise, reference intakes are based on an average-sized woman doing an average amount of physical activity. This is to reduce the risk of those with lower energy requirements eating too much and to make sure information on labels is clear and consistent.

HOW CAN YOU TELL IF A FOOD IS HIGH IN FAT, SATURATED FAT, SUGARS OR SALT?

Fat
High in fat: more than 17.5g per 100g

Low in fat: 3g or less per 100g

Saturated fat (saturates)
High in saturates: more than 5g per 100g

Low in saturates: 1.5g or less per 100g

Sugars
High in sugars: more than 22.5g per 100g

Low in sugars: 5g or less per 100g

Salt
High in salt: more than 1.5g per 100g

Low in salt: 0.3g or less per 100g

The red, amber and green colour coding on the front of packs helps you see at a glance whether a food is high (red), medium (amber) or low (green) in fat, saturated fat, sugars or salt.

Where to find reference intakes on food packs?
If you look closely at food packaging, you'll see that it usually tells you what percentage of your daily reference intakes each portion of that food contains.

Each portion contains:

Energy	Fat	Saturates	Sugars	Salt
126kJ	**12.5g**	**0.0g**	**3.8g**	**2.04g**
30kcals				
2%	**18%**	**0%**	**4%**	**33%**

Of your reference intake

The food label above shows that:

- Each portion will provide you with 2.04g salt, which is 33% of your daily reference intake for salt.

- The red colour shows you that the item is high in salt.

- The item also contains 12.5g of fat, which is 18% of your reference intake for fat.

- The amber colour tells you that the item contains a medium amount of fat.

- Green means a food is low in a particular nutrient; this item is low in saturated fat and sugar.

RECIPES

BASIC RECIPES

Stocks
Chicken

Fish

Vegetable

Soup
Velvety vegetable

Rustic tomato

Chicken

Minestrone with borlotti beans

Eggs
Soft-boiled

Fried

Scrambled

Poached

Ramekin

Omelette

Chilli

Pasta
Dried

Fresh

Rice
Plain boiled

Braised

Pilau

Risotto

Vanilla rice pudding with mango compote

Pulses
Scottish lentil soup

Homemade hummus

Homemade baked beans on toast

Grains
Couscous salad with herbs and pomegranate

Vegetables
Blanching: a tomato

Roasting: squash with thyme and garlic

Grilling: cauliflower cheese

Braising: red cabbage

Deep-frying: onion rings

Shallow-frying: courgettes

Stir-frying: Chinese vegetables

Stewing: ratatouille

Potatoes
Boiled

Baked potatoes in their jackets

Mash

Chips

Braised

Perfect roasties

Poultry
Braised chicken legs with mushrooms

Grilled chicken

Roast chicken

Sweet and sour chicken

Lemon and Parmesan chicken

Chicken curry with saffron and almonds

Fish
Cured salmon with soy lemon dressing

Baked cod with parsley crust

Pan-fried mackerel with pomegranate and honey dressing

Poached salmon

Grilled fillets of sole

Meat
Mutton shepherd's pie

Grilled lamb chops

Spaghetti Bolognese

Baked toad in the hole

Beef burgers

Roast pork belly with caramelised apples and mustard sauce

Boiled bacon

Beef bourguignon

Pan-fried steak

Sauces & dressings
Basic tomato sauce

Rich tomato sauce

Pesto

Vinaigrette

Gravy

White sauce

Bread
Basic white

Honey and hempseed

ADDITIONAL RECIPES

Sharing Food

Pizza

Thai curry & satay + chicken satay

Indian spiced glazed chicken wings + chickpea curry

Grilled corn with chilli & feta + sticky ribs

Beef tacos & Mexican coleslaw

Prawn stir-fry + tempura vegetables with sherry soy dipping sauce

Lemon drizzle popcorn + chocolate brownie

Breakfast

Banana and raspberry smoothie with Greek yoghurt and honey

Apple, lemon and honey muesli with raspberries and almonds

Poached eggs on toast with grilled bacon

Simple bagels with scrambled egg and plum tomatoes

Very fruity compote with yoghurt

Super berry, cinnamon and honey granola

Lunch

Hearty chicken and pasta soup

Roasted peppers with goat's cheese

Avocado and pasta salad with flaxseed

Carrot, coconut and almond soup

Beetroot, feta and walnut salad

Dinner

Chef's risotto with peas and mint

Seared salmon with soy greens

Garlic roasted chicken with roasted carrots, potatoes and gravy

Chicken and vegetable stir-fry with noodles

Healthy lamb burger

Puddings

Espresso nectarines

Orange and rosehip yoghurt sorbet

Fruit salad with elderflower meringues

Blueberry jelly with Prosecco topped with Greek yoghurt and honey

Garden ginger and rhubarb crumble

Chocolate pot with orange marmalade salsa

STOCKS

Stocks are the basis of many dishes. To be honest, not many people make them from scratch. You can buy stock cubes, jellies and fresh stock. But are they as good? Well, no, most of them taste pretty awful, are too salty and contain unnecessary ingredients.

So why not create your own? And they'll save you money, because you can use up certain ingredients that you might otherwise throw away, such as the carcass of the roast chicken you had on Sunday.

Here are three simple recipes in which you can substitute ingredients that you have to hand.

WHITE OR BROWN CHICKEN STOCK

STUFF YOU'LL NEED

1 carcass of a raw or cooked chicken

2 litres/8½ cups water

1 carrot, cut into quarters

1 onion, cut into quarters

1 stick of celery, cut into quarters

1 leek, cut into quarters

2 sprigs fresh thyme

5 peppercorns

Note: for a brown stock, roast the bones in a hot oven until they are well coloured and add a tbsp of tomato purée.

GET STUCK IN

1 Chop the bones up into two or three pieces.

2 Place the bones in a pot with the water and bring it to the boil.

3 Once boiling, turn down to a simmer and add the vegetables, herbs and peppercorns, and simmer for a couple of hours.

4 Strain and boil to reduce by half to strengthen the flavour.

5 Cover with cling film and cool completely before refrigerating or freezing.

MAKES 1.5 LITRES/6¼ CUPS

Each portion contains:

Energy	Fat	Saturates	Sugars	Salt
126kJ 30kcals	0.2g	0.0g	3.8g	0.0g
2%	0%	0%	4%	0%

Of your reference intake

FISH STOCK

STUFF YOU'LL NEED

20g/^{1}/$_8$ cup butter

1 onion, sliced

1 or 2 white fish carcasses, chopped

1 litre/4¼ cups water

1 lemon

5 peppercorns

Parsley stalks

GET STUCK IN

1 Melt the butter and add the onion, cooking gently for a couple of minutes.

2 Wash the fish bones and add to the onion, stirring from time to time.

3 Add the water and bring to the boil, turning down as soon as it starts bubbling. Add the lemon, peppercorns and parsley.

4 Simmer for 15 minutes and strain through a fine sieve.

5 Place in another pot and bring to the boil, then boil down by half to strengthen the flavour.

6 Cover with cling film and cool completely before refrigerating or freezing.

MAKES 1 LITRE/4¼ CUPS

Each portion contains:

Energy	Fat	Saturates	Sugars	Salt
260kJ	**4.3g**	**2.6g**	**2.2g**	**0.1g**
62kcals				
3%	6%	13%	2%	2%

Of your reference intake

VEGETABLE STOCK

STUFF YOU'LL NEED

1 onion, diced

1 carrot, diced

1 stick of celery, diced

1 leek, cut in half and diced

1 handful of mushrooms, quartered

1 tbsp olive oil

3 tomatoes, cut into quarters

1 tsp tomato purée

10 peppercorns

2 sprigs fresh thyme

Parsley stalks

GET STUCK IN

1 Heat a pan and fry the vegetables in the olive oil until lightly golden.

2 Add the tomatoes, the tomato purée, peppercorns, thyme and the parsley stalks, stir well, cover with cold water and bring to the boil. Turn down to a simmer and gently cook for 25 minutes.

3 Take off the heat, cover with cling film and leave to cool.

4 Once cooled, strain and refrigerate or freeze.

MAKES 1.5 LITRES/6¼ CUPS

Each portion contains:

Energy	Fat	Saturates	Sugars	Salt
1053kJ 253kcals	12.1g	1.8g	22.1g	0.13g
13%	17%	9%	25%	2%

Of your reference intake

SOUP

Soups are a fantastic way to incorporate more vegetables into your diet and can often make a meal in themselves. For me, they're a way of looking after myself using food and evoke a lot of emotional memories. When I am feeling lonely, I'll eat a lovely velvety vegetable soup, as it reminds me of my grandmother. If I'm unwell, I will dig a chicken soup out of the freezer and add plenty of chopped parsley to it.

This takes me right back to my parents' house and makes me feel like my mother is looking after me.

Soup has to be one of the most vital foods as it is very nutritious. I think that learning to make different varieties is as important as learning to make bread. If it's about survival and basic living, then soup and bread will get you to the next post every time.

VELVETY VEGETABLE SOUP

STUFF YOU'LL NEED

1 onion

1 leek

1 carrot

1 stick of celery

2 big handfuls of other vegetables such as squash, asparagus, mushrooms, cauliflower, parsnips, turnips and beetroot – whatever's in your fridge

200g/¾ cup butter

30g/¼ cup plain flour

1 litre/4¼ cups chicken stock (see page 60)

300ml/1¼ cups double cream

1 sprig fresh thyme

Salt and freshly ground black pepper

GET STUCK IN

1 Peel and chop all the vegetables and cook them in the butter without colouring. Place a lid on the pan to help them steam and cook quicker.

2 Add the flour and mix in, then cook for 2–3 minutes more.

3 Gradually pour in the hot stock, stirring until it reaches the boil.

4 Add the cream, thyme and season to taste and bring back to the boil, then simmer for 20 minutes more or until the vegetables are cooked through.

5 Take the pan off the heat and blend until really smooth.

6 Strain the soup and check the seasoning.

MAKES 1 LITRE/4¼ CUPS

Each portion contains:

Energy	Fat	Saturates	Sugars	Salt
1179kJ 282kcals	18.7g	11.4g	7.0g	<0.1g
14%	27%	57%	8%	11%

Of your reference intake

RUSTIC TOMATO SOUP

STUFF YOU'LL NEED

100ml/7 tbsp extra virgin olive oil

1 onion, finely chopped

2 cloves garlic, smashed

100g/¾ cup plain flour

100g/2 tbsp tomato purée

1 litre/4¼ cups vegetable stock (see page 62)

2 x 400g/14oz tins peeled plum tomatoes, chopped

1 sprig fresh rosemary, chopped

Salt and freshly ground black pepper

3 slices of an old loaf of bread

20g/¼ cup Parmesan cheese, grated

GET STUCK IN

1 Warm half the olive oil in a pan, add the onion and garlic and soften without colouring too much.

2 Mix in the flour and stir well. Cook for a couple of minutes.

3 Add the tomato purée and mix in whilst adding the hot stock.

4 Add the plum tomatoes and bring to the boil, then add the chopped rosemary leaves and season with salt and pepper. Simmer for 20 minutes or so.

5 Preheat the oven to 180°C/350°F/gas 4. Rip up the bread and place on an oven tray.

6 Drizzle with the remaining extra virgin olive oil and seasoning, then bake in the oven for 8–10 minutes or until golden brown. Serve with the soup.

7 Add some grated Parmesan if you fancy it.

MAKES 1 LITRE/4¼ CUPS

Each portion contains:

Energy	Fat	Saturates	Sugars	Salt
794kJ 190kcals	13.0g	2.1g	4.2g	2.9g
10%	19%	10%	4%	48%

Of your reference intake

CHICKEN SOUP

STUFF YOU'LL NEED

1 small 1.5kg/3lb 5oz chicken, roasted for an hour

4 carrots, diced

2 onions, diced

200g/1 cup barley

Freshly ground black pepper

2 sprigs fresh thyme

3 litres/12¾ cups chicken stock (see page 60)

1 big handful of fresh parsley, chopped

GET STUCK IN

1 Place all the ingredients in a pan, apart from the parsley.

2 Bring to the boil, then turn down the heat and simmer for 1 hour.

3 Turn the heat off and cover until cold.

4 Once cold, take out the chicken, pull the meat off the bone and reserve.

5 Warm the liquid, add the chicken and freshly chopped parsley.

Note: if you are making this to freeze, freeze in portions with the added chicken and parsley. Defrost and reheat appropriately at a later stage.

MAKES 2 LITRES/8½ CUPS

Each portion contains:

Energy	Fat	Saturates	Sugars	Salt
1411kJ **200kcals**	**15.5g**	**4.2g**	**2.9g**	**0.8g**
10%	**22%**	**21%**	**3%**	**14%**

Of your reference intake

MINESTRONE WITH BORLOTTI BEANS

STUFF YOU'LL NEED

100ml/7 tbsp olive oil

125g/4½oz pancetta or streaky bacon, diced

1 onion, diced

1 leek, diced

2 carrots, diced

1 turnip, diced

1 cabbage, diced

2 sprigs fresh thyme

150g/3 tbsp tomato purée

50g/1¾oz borlotti beans, soaked overnight in water

2 litres/8½ cups chicken stock (see page 60)

60g/2oz spaghetti, snapped into 3cm /1¼in pieces

100g/3½oz potatoes, peeled and diced

50g/⅓ cup French beans, chopped

50g/½ cup peas

1 x 400g/14oz tin chopped plum tomatoes

Salt and freshly ground black pepper

1 handful of fresh parsley, chopped

50g/½ cup Parmesan cheese, grated

GET STUCK IN

1 In a large pan, heat the olive oil and cook the pancetta until coloured slightly.

2 Add the vegetables and continue on a medium heat with the lid on.

3 Add the thyme, tomato purée, borlotti beans and the stock. Cook for 20 minutes or so, simmering all the time.

4 Add the spaghetti and potatoes to the soup.

5 Continue to cook for 5 minutes or until they are cooked.

6 Add the chopped French beans, peas and chopped tomatoes. Bring to the boil and season with salt and pepper.

7 Add the parsley and sprinkle with grated Parmesan cheese to serve.

MAKES 1.5 LITRES/6¼ CUPS

Each portion contains:

Energy	Fat	Saturates	Sugars	Salt
625kJ 151kcals	10.5g	2.3g	2.7g	2.5g
8%	15%	11%	3%	42%

Of your reference intake

EGGS

Eggs are an important part of our diet; the white contains significant amounts of protein and choline, which are both very good for us. The yolk is high in saturated fat, so I'd say eating three or four eggs a week is a good amount for our bodies. Of course, there are loads of different types to choose from: hen, duck and quail eggs are widely used, but goose, turkey and guinea fowl eggs are also really great to try.

Eggs are really versatile, and here I've outlined some of the simplest ways to cook them. I learned these recipes when I was young, and I have to say that I will never go hungry again.

It's important that all eggs are fresh and stored in a cool, dark place.

SOFT-BOILED EGGS

STUFF YOU'LL NEED

Allow 1 or 2 eggs per person

Water

Butter

Allow 1 or 2 slices bread per person, toasted and buttered

Salt and freshly ground black pepper

GET STUCK IN

1 Place the eggs in cold water in a small saucepan and bring to the boil.

2 Start the timer as soon as the water begins to boil properly and boil for 3 minutes, then remove the eggs from the water with a spoon.

3 Peel off the top of the eggshell.

4 Serve with hot buttered toast and a small pinch of salt and pepper on top of the egg.

Each portion contains:

Energy	Fat	Saturates	Sugars	Salt
612kJ 147kcals	10.8g	3.1g	0g	0.4g
7%	15%	16%	0%	7%

Of your reference intake

FRIED EGGS

STUFF YOU'LL NEED

A small knob of butter or 1 tsp sunflower oil

Allow 1 or 2 eggs per person

Salt and freshly ground black pepper

GET STUCK IN

1 Melt the butter or warm the oil in a frying pan.

2 Break the eggs carefully into a cup or small bowl without breaking the yolk, then tip them gently into the frying pan.

3 Cook gently until lightly set, then season with salt and pepper.

4 Drain with a fish slice and serve on a plate.

Each portion contains:

Energy	Fat	Saturates	Sugars	Salt
878kJ 211kcals	16.8g	6.2g	0g	0.5g
11%	24%	31%	0%	8%

Of your reference intake

SCRAMBLED EGGS

STUFF YOU'LL NEED

Allow 1 or 2 eggs per person

Salt and freshly ground black pepper

A knob of butter

20ml/1½ tbsp double cream for every 2 eggs

GET STUCK IN

1 Break the eggs into a bowl, season with salt and pepper and whisk with a fork.

2 Melt the butter in a non-stick, heavy pan. Add the eggs and cook over a gentle heat, stirring continuously until the eggs start to set. Continue to stir until the eggs are lightly cooked through.

3 Take off the heat and pour in a little cold double cream. This stops the cooking process. Adjust the seasoning if needed, and serve.

Each portion contains:

Energy	Fat	Saturates	Sugars	Salt
1341kJ 325kcals	30.2g	15.0g	0g	0.5g
16%	43%	75%	0%	8%

Of your reference intake

POACHED EGGS

Salt

Water

A little white vinegar

Very fresh eggs, allow
1 or 2 per person

GET STUCK IN

1 In a fairly deep saucepan, bring some salted water to the boil. Add the vinegar and return to a gentle boil.

2 Carefully break the eggs into a ramekin and gently tip into the softly rolling water.

3 Poach at just under the boil until lightly set. This takes about 3–4 minutes. You want the yolk to be still soft to touch but encased by the set white.

4 Remove with a slotted spoon and place in iced water. Trim the white if you would like a more finished look to your eggs.

5 Once you have cooked all your eggs, reheat as you need them by placing in hot salted water for a minute or so. Drain before placing on a serving plate.

Each portion contains:

Energy	Fat	Saturates	Sugars	Salt
657kJ 158kcals	10.8g	3.0g	0.0g	0.5g
8%	15%	15%	0%	8%

Of your reference intake

RAMEKIN EGGS

25g/¹/₈ cup butter

Salt and freshly ground black pepper

Allow 1 or 2 eggs per person

Allow 1 or 2 slices bread per person, toasted and buttered

GET STUCK IN

1 Leaving some for the toast, butter some ovenproof ramekins and season.

2 Break two eggs carefully into each ramekin and season.

3 Place the ramekins in a frying pan containing 1cm/1/3in of water.

4 Put a tight-fitting lid on top of the frying pan and place on a high heat, so that the water starts to boil rapidly.

5 Cook for 2–3 minutes or until the egg whites are lightly set but the yolk remains soft.

6 Serve with hot buttered toast.

Each portion contains:

Energy	Fat	Saturates	Sugars	Salt
966kJ **233kcals**	**19.0g**	**8.2g**	**0.0g**	**1.63g**
12%	**27%**	**41%**	**0%**	**6%**

Of your reference intake

OMELETTE

3 eggs

Salt and freshly ground black pepper

1 tbsp sunflower oil

A knob of butter

GET STUCK IN

1 Break the eggs into a bowl and season with salt and pepper. Whisk well with a fork.

2 Heat a non-stick omelette pan or small frying pan on a high heat for a minute or so.

3 Add the oil and butter and heat until it starts foaming but not colouring.

4 Add the whisked eggs and mix quickly using the fork or a rubber spatula until they are lightly set.

5 Remove from the heat.

6 Fold over so one edge meets the middle and repeat on the other side.

7 Tap the pan handle so that the omelette hops to the edge of the pan. Carefully tilt the pan over so that the omelette falls into the centre of the serving plate.

8 Neaten the shape if necessary. Chefs look for a cigar shape. Serve immediately.

Note: you can obviously add lots of different ingredients to an omelette – before folding it up. I love smoked salmon, ham, cheese, mushrooms or fresh herbs.

Each portion contains:

Energy	Fat	Saturates	Sugars	Salt
1329kJ **320kcals**	**25.3g**	**7.8g**	**0.0g**	**2.6g**
16%	36%	39%	0%	46%

Of your reference intake

CHILLI EGGS

STUFF YOU'LL NEED

1 tbsp olive oil

1 onion, chopped

1 clove garlic, chopped

1 large red chilli, deseeded and finely chopped

1 x 400g/14oz tin red kidney beans, drained and rinsed

4 fresh plum tomatoes, chopped

1 x 400g/14oz tin plum tomatoes, chopped

1 tsp sugar

Salt and freshly ground black pepper

4 eggs

1 small handful of fresh coriander, chopped

Sour cream, to serve

Warm tortilla chips

GET STUCK IN

1 Heat the olive oil in a deep frying pan and cook the onion, garlic and chilli on a medium heat for 3–4 minutes until soft but not brown. Add the beans and fresh chopped tomatoes and stir-fry for a few minutes.

2 Add the tinned tomatoes and sugar and turn down to a low heat to simmer for 5–10 minutes.

3 Once thickened, season to taste.

4 Make 4 even holes in the now-thickened sauce and crack an egg into each one. Cover and simmer over a low heat for 5 or so minutes until the egg whites are set and the yolks are still runny. Cook for longer if you prefer your eggs cooked through.

5 Sprinkle with the chopped coriander and serve with the a bowl of sour cream and some warm tortilla chips.

Each portion contains:

Energy	Fat	Saturates	Sugars	Salt
1760kJ 419kcals	18.7g	3.7g	19.4g	1.8g
21%	27%	18.5%	21.5%	17%

Of your reference intake

PASTA

I am from Italian stock. My mum's father was Italian and therefore pasta has always played an important part in my life.

Not all Italians eat fresh pasta every day. Dried pasta is perfectly good, so I've included instructions for both dried and freshly made pasta.

Pasta is made from wheat called durum, which is a strong flour that is very starchy and full of carbohydrates. It's great for building energy within your body, so it's especially good if you are doing a lot of exercise or hard physical work.

For pasta sauces, see the sauces and dressing section on page 148.

DRIED PASTA

STUFF YOU'LL NEED

Enough water to cover the pasta well

Salt

A splash of olive oil

100g/3½oz pasta per portion

GET STUCK IN

1 Bring the water to the boil and add the salt and olive oil.

2 Add the pasta in small quantities to avoid sticking.

3 Once it's all added, bring back to the boil and stir occasionally.

4 Boil until the pasta is 'al dente', meaning 'to the tooth', i.e. firm but tender. It should have a little bite to it but be cooked through.

5 Drain but do not rinse, unless you want the pasta to be cold. If the sauce is a little thick, you can reserve some cooking water to loosen up the sauce. It contains the natural starch from the pasta.

Note: you can get many different shapes of pasta and they take different times to cook, so follow the instructions on the packet. If you need to reheat pasta, simply add it to a pan of boiling, salted water with a splash of olive oil to prevent it sticking together. Heat for 2–3 minutes and drain in a colander.

Each portion contains:

Energy 1567kJ 373kcals	Fat 13.4g	Saturates 1.6g	Sugars 1.4g	Salt 0.1g
19%	19%	8%	2%	2%

Of your reference intake

FRESH PASTA

STUFF YOU'LL NEED

175g/1⅔ cups pasta flour
(sometimes labelled
'00' flour)

1 whole egg

2 egg yolks

1 tsp water

GET STUCK IN

1 Place all the ingredients in a food processor and mix quickly to form a wet crumb. This only takes 30 seconds.

2 Form a ball of dough in your hands and, using a dusting of flour, knead until smooth. You need to work the dough to stretch the gluten. This will avoid shrinkage when rolling out and cooking. You will know when you have a nice dough because it will be very smooth to the touch.

3 Rest the dough for at least 30 minutes.

4 Roll pieces of dough out into very thin sheets and cut lengthways into the desired strip widths.

5 Cook the fresh pasta like the dried but for just 2–3 minutes. Once you have placed it in the water, bring it back to the boil and then strain.

Note: the easiest way to roll out pasta is to use a pasta machine. Once you have mastered fresh pasta, try adding flavours using cooked purées such as spinach, tomato or beetroot. The purée would replace the water and whole egg.

MAKES 2 PORTIONS

Each portion contains:

Energy	Fat	Saturates	Sugars	Salt
1682kJ	**8.7g**	**2.4g**	**1.5g**	**<0.1g**
399kcals				
20%	**12%**	**12%**	**2%**	**2%**

Of your reference intake

RICE

Rice is one of the most important crops in the world and grows in some of its most beautiful places. Sunshine and rain is a must to grow the lush green plants that spur the rice grain.

There are hundreds of varieties, including short, long, brown, white and red. Different countries like different types. Italians love Arborio. Asian and Indian countries use mainly basmati, while Europeans and Americans use the long-grain, pudding and wild rice.

Note that rice is a very useful, fairly inexpensive carbohydrate. Be careful not to keep it hot for longer than two hours and reheat it only once.

PLAIN BOILED RICE

STUFF YOU'LL NEED

80g/½ cup
long-grain rice
per person

Salt

Water to cover
the rice well

GET STUCK IN

1 Wash the rice under cold running water.

2 Add the rice to plenty of boiling salted water.

3 Stir, bring back to the boil, turn down the heat and simmer for 12 minutes until tender.

4 Pour into a sieve and rinse well under cold running water and then boiling water.

5 Place in a bowl and cover with a cloth.

Each portion contains:

Energy	Fat	Saturates	Sugars	Salt
1222kJ 291kcals	0.8g	0g	0g	0g
15%	1%	0%	0%	0%

Of your reference intake

BRAISED RICE

STUFF YOU'LL NEED

50g/¼ cup butter

1 onion, finely chopped

300g/1⅔ cups long-grain rice

600ml/2½ cups white chicken or vegetable stock (see pages 60 & 62)

1 sprig fresh thyme

Salt and freshly ground black pepper

A knob of butter, to serve

GET STUCK IN

1 Preheat the oven to 220°C/425°F/gas 7.

2 Warm the butter in a pan and add the onion, cooking slowly without colouring it.

3 Add the rice and cook gently for a couple of minutes.

4 Add the stock to the rice, then the thyme and seasoning, then cover and bring to the boil.

5 Put in the oven for 15 minutes until cooked.

6 Add a knob of butter to serve.

Each portion contains:

Energy	Fat	Saturates	Sugars	Salt
1722kJ 410kcals	22.8g	13.5g	2.2g	1.3g
20%	33%	68%	2%	22%

Of your reference intake

PILAU RICE

STUFF YOU'LL NEED

300g/1⅔ cups basmati rice

1 tbsp butter

2 bay leaves

1 tsp turmeric

5 cloves

5 cardamom pods

1 cinnamon stick

1 tsp fennel seeds

1 tsp cumin seeds

1 star anise

600ml/2½ cups boiling water

50g/½ cup toasted flaked almonds

50g/¼ cup sultanas

GET STUCK IN

1 Wash and drain the rice.

2 Heat the butter in a large saucepan and fry the spices for a minute.

3 Add the rice and stir-fry for a minute.

4 Add the boiling water and stir in the almonds and sultanas.

5 Place a lid on top and turn down to the lowest heat.

6 Leave for 8 minutes, after which the water should be completely absorbed.

7 Check the rice is cooked and remove from the heat when it is ready.

8 Fluff the rice with a fork and serve.

MAKES 4 PORTIONS

Each portion contains:

Energy	Fat	Saturates	Sugars	Salt
1780kJ **422kcals**	**10.8g**	**2.5g**	**8.9g**	**0.08g**
21%	15%	12%	10%	1%

Of your reference intake

RISOTTO

STUFF YOU'LL NEED

1 litre/4¼ cups white chicken or vegetable stock (see pages 60 & 62)

70g/⅓ cup butter

1 onion, finely chopped

1 clove garlic, crushed

1 sprig fresh thyme

200g/1 cup Arborio rice

60g/¾ cup Parmesan cheese, grated

Salt and freshly ground black pepper

GET STUCK IN

1 Bring the stock to the boil. Leave it near to where you are going to cook the risotto.

2 In another pan, heat half the butter and cook the onion, garlic and thyme until it softens, do not colour.

3 Add the rice and stir-fry with a spatula for a few minutes.

4 Add a ladle of stock and stir it in. Continue to cook until the stock is absorbed.

5 Add the stock a ladleful at a time, cooking until the stock is absorbed. The rice will start to expand as it cooks. It should be tender when finished and it usually takes about 20 minutes after the first ladle of stock.

6 When it's cooked, take it off the stove, stir in the other half of the butter and half of the Parmesan cheese. Season to taste and cover.

7 Serve after the risotto has rested for a minute or two. Sprinkle with the remaining Parmesan cheese.

MAKES 2 PORTIONS

Each portion contains:

Energy	Fat	Saturates	Sugars	Salt
1974kJ 470kcals	38.5g	24.0g	2.5g	3.4g
24%	55%	120%	3%	57%

Of your reference intake

VANILLA RICE PUDDING WITH MANGO COMPOTE

STUFF YOU'LL NEED

100g/½ cup short-grain pudding rice

1 vanilla pod

1.2 litres/5 cups semi-skimmed milk

100g/½ cup caster sugar

100ml/7 tbsp double cream

Icing sugar, for dusting

For the compote

100g/¾ cup icing sugar

100ml/7 tbsp water

1 star anise

1 tsp ground cinnamon

1 Indian mango

GET STUCK IN

1 Wash and drain the rice. Split the vanilla pod in half and scrape out all the seeds.

2 In a large heavy pan, place the milk, sugar and vanilla seeds and pod. Bring to the boil.

3 Turn the milk down to a simmer, add the rice and cook for 30 minutes.

4 Now make the compote: in another small pan, mix the sugar, water, star anise and cinnamon. Bring to the boil.

5 Slice the mango into two halves, either side of the stone and as near to the stone as you can get. Take each half and score lengthways and across down to the peel so that when you bend the peel backwards, the squares of mango sit up like a hedgehog. Carefully cut the squares of mango away from the peel and then add them to the stock syrup until they become soft but still have a slight bite.

6 Remove from the heat and allow to cool and thicken.

7 Once the rice is fully cooked, correct the consistency with as much cream as needed.

8 To serve, place the rice in a shallow bowl and put a dessertspoon of mango compote on top.

9 Dust with icing sugar.

MAKES 4 PORTIONS

Each portion contains:

Energy	Fat	Saturates	Sugars	Salt
2331kJ 555kcals	19.0g	11.6g	64.3g	0.4g
28%	27%	58%	71%	7%

Of your reference intake

PULSES

Pulses are a very versatile ingredient and can be used in all manner of dishes. They're particularly good for vegetarian dishes, as they're high in protein and can be really tasty.

Most pulses are low in fat and high in vitamin B. The other great thing about pulses is that they're cheap and easy to store, making them a great store-cupboard ingredient.

All the pulses listed on the next page are unique and amazing in their own way. It's well worth trying different ones and mixing them up. Together, they can make an array of different flavours, textures and colours.

HERE ARE SOME OF THE PULSES THAT CAN BE INCLUDED IN YOUR COOKING VERY EASILY

Beans: aduki, black, black-eyed, borlotti, broad, butter, cannellini, flageolet and haricot, mung, pinto, red kidney and soy

Peas: chickpeas, red and yellow split peas

Lentils: brown, dhal, green, Indian, orange, puy, red and yellow

GENERAL COOKING OF PULSES

STUFF YOU'LL NEED

60g/¼ cup dried pulses per person

GET STUCK IN

Dried pulses need to be soaked, but for varying times, so it's best to check the individual packet for instructions.

Cook in boiling, salted water until cooked, following the instructions on the packet. Taste to check they are cooked – they should be tender with no bite when chewed. Stop the cooking process by chilling in cold water.

SCOTTISH LENTIL SOUP

STUFF YOU'LL NEED

340g/1¾ cups red split lentils

30g/⅛ cup butter

4 slices back bacon, finely sliced

2 medium onions, finely diced

3 carrots, finely diced

3 sticks of celery, finely diced

2 cloves garlic, roughly chopped

1.5 litres/6¼ cups water

1 bay leaf

1 handful of fresh parsley, chopped

Salt and freshly ground black pepper

GET STUCK IN

1 Wash the lentils in a sieve under cold running water.

2 Tip into a bowl, cover with warm water and soak for 30 minutes.

3 Heat the butter in a large pan and fry the bacon until it is lightly coloured.

4 Mix in the vegetables and garlic and fry until soft. Drain the lentils and mix into the vegetables.

5 Add the water and bay leaf and simmer gently for about 30 minutes or until the lentils are soft.

6 Skim off any scum that rises to the surface.

7 When cooked, liquidise until smooth, return to a clean pan, add the chopped parsley and season to taste.

MAKES 6 PORTIONS

Each portion contains:

Energy	Fat	Saturates	Sugars	Salt
1295kJ	8.5g	4.0g	6.5g	1.19g
308kcals				
15%	12%	20%	7%	20%

Of your reference intake

HOMEMADE HUMMUS

STUFF YOU'LL NEED

250g/1½ cups dried chickpeas

1 tsp bicarbonate of soda

Salt and freshly ground black pepper

4 cloves garlic, crushed

8 tbsp Greek yoghurt

2 lemons, zested and juiced

1 tsp paprika

GET STUCK IN

1 Rinse the dried chickpeas and soak for 10 hours in cold water with the bicarbonate of soda, which helps them to soften quicker.

2 When ready to cook, rinse again, place in a pot and cover with water. Bring to the boil, turn down the heat and simmer for about an hour or until the chickpeas are soft enough to crush with your fingers easily.

3 Once cooked, and while still hot, drain in a sieve over a bowl, saving a little of the water. Put the chickpeas into a food processor, add some salt and the garlic and slowly start the machine to turn the chickpeas into a purée. Add a little water to help break down the chickpeas if necessary.

4 Add the yoghurt, lemon zest and juice and paprika whilst turning.

5 Taste the hummus and check for seasoning and balance of flavour.

MAKES 4 PORTIONS

Each portion contains:

Energy	Fat	Saturates	Sugars	Salt
1394kJ 332kcals	12.8g	6.5g	7.2g	0.3g
17%	18%	32%	8%	5%

Of your reference intake

HOMEMADE BAKED BEANS ON TOAST

STUFF YOU'LL NEED

110g/⅔ cup dried haricots blanc beans

1 small onion, peeled

4 cloves

6 peppercorns

1 bay leaf

4 sage leaves

6 cloves garlic, peeled

20g/⅛ cup tomato purée

1 x 400g/14oz tin chopped tomatoes

1 tomato, peeled, deseeded and diced

Salt and freshly ground black pepper

4 slices bread, toasted and buttered, to serve

GET STUCK IN

1 Place the beans in a large bowl, cover with cold water and leave to soak overnight.

2 Next day, preheat the oven to 160°C/320°F/gas 3, drain and rinse the beans under cold running water. Place in a large ovenproof dish or baking tin with enough cold water to cover.

3 Pierce the onion with the cloves and add to the beans with the peppercorns, bay leaf, sage, garlic, half of the tomato purée and the tinned tomatoes. Bring to the boil on the stove, then cover and place in the oven for 2–3 hours until the beans are quite soft. Check the beans aren't drying out from time to time and add a little boiling water if they are.

4 Remove the bay leaf, onion and cloves. Add the diced tomato and remaining tomato purée, stir and cook for a further 30 minutes. Season to taste and serve on warm buttered toast.

5 You can easily add a poached egg (see page 71) and grated Cheddar.

MAKES 4 PORTIONS

Each portion contains:

Energy	Fat	Saturates	Sugars	Salt
487kJ	0.8g	0.1g	5.9g	0.2g
114kcals				
6%	1%	1%	6%	3%

Of your reference intake

GRAINS

Cereal crops or grains are, in essence, grasses. They are cut, cultivated and the grains or seeds are used as edible food.

They're produced in massive yields, known as 'staple crops', and they produce more energy than any other harvested crop. Grains are rich in carbohydrates and supply most of their energy as starch. They're also a huge source of protein.

Grains are full of fibre and nutrients, so they are a really good source of food and should be included as part of your healthy diet.

HERE ARE SOME OF THE GRAINS THAT YOU CAN INCLUDE IN YOUR COOKING

rice (see page 78)

barley, buckwheat, corn or maize, millet, oats and rye

couscous, quinoa, spelt and wheat

GENERAL COOKING OF GRAINS

STUFF YOU'LL NEED

60g/⅓ cup dried grains per person

GET STUCK IN

1 Remember to use a heavy saucepan with a tight-fitting lid. Rinse the grains thoroughly. Follow the instructions on the packet regarding grain-to-water ratio. Bring the water to the boil, add the grain and a good pinch of salt, and return to the boil. Turn down the heat, cover and simmer for the indicated time.

2 Stop the cooking process by chilling in cold water.

COUSCOUS SALAD WITH HERBS AND POMEGRANATE

STUFF YOU'LL NEED

200g/1 cup couscous

200ml/¾ cup boiling water

1 pomegranate

1 handful of fresh mint and coriander, ripped up

1 orange, zested and juiced

2 tbsp white wine vinegar

6 tbsp olive oil

Salt and freshly ground black pepper

GET STUCK IN

1 Place the couscous in a shallow bowl, then pour over the boiling water. Cover the bowl with cling film, then leave for 5 minutes until the couscous has swelled up and absorbed the water.

2 Meanwhile, cut the pomegranate in half (widthways). Hold over a bowl and, using a rolling pin, knock the seeds out.

3 Fluff the couscous with a fork to separate the grains, and then stir through the pomegranate seeds and herbs.

4 Make a dressing by mixing together the orange juice and zest, vinegar and olive oil, then stir into the couscous. Season to taste.

MAKES 4 PORTIONS

Each portion contains:

Energy	Fat	Saturates	Sugars	Salt
1635kJ 391kcals	23.6g	3.4g	2.1g	<0.01g
20%	34%	17%	2%	0%

Of your reference intake

VEGETABLES

Now, I know it's stating the obvious to say that vegetables are hugely important in our diet, but what exactly are they?

They are, in general, the edible part of plants. There are some plants we treat as vegetables that, strictly speaking, belong to other groups. One example is the mushroom, which technically belongs to the 'fungi' family. And guess what? Tomatoes are actually fruit! But I will include both as vegetables in this section for simplicity.

Vegetables are full of vitamins, minerals and carbohydrates and can be used in so many ways – they're ultra-versatile. Vegetables grown under the ground are called 'root vegetables'. These also contain starch and sugar – a good source of energy – and they also have small but powerful quantities of protein.

Green vegetables are rich in mineral salts and vitamins, particularly vitamin C and carotene. The greener the leaf, the more vitamins it contains. The main minerals are calcium and iron. So now you know where the phrase 'eat your greens' came from!

To get the most out of your vegetables, you need to eat them at their optimum freshness and at the height of their season. However, that doesn't mean you can't do fantastic things with vegetables that are not at their best, so don't be put off by a wilting cabbage. What is true to say is that overcooked vegetables have definitely lost their goodness, so eating your vegetables either raw or only just cooked is by far the best way to maximise their value to you.

PREPARING AND COOKING YOUR VEGETABLES: A ROUGH GUIDE

Most people overcook their vegetables, although they are starting to learn that vegetables should have texture when they're served on the plate.

Try not to store them too long, as they will start to lose their goodness and dry out. Just buy what you need for the week.

Shop in a market at the end of the day to get the best deals. Don't be fooled by supermarket deals; markets are generally cheaper every time.

Generally, vegetables grown underground are cooked initially in cold water, whereas vegetables grown above the ground are cooked in boiling, salted water and as quickly as possible. You can stop the cooking process with iced water, if available. This will maximise the goodness and help to keep their colour and texture too. This is called blanching and refreshing. Vegetables can also be cooked using most of the other methods explained in this book.

CUTS

Understanding how to cut vegetables is useful if you want to work in catering, and it can help in home cooking if you're using professional cookery books. The size and shape varies depending on the natural type, shape and size of each vegetable, but on the page opposite is a list of the classic cuts.

COOKING VEGETABLES

To help understand the cooking process, I've listed some good examples. It's a vast area and you can use most cooking methods with most vegetables.

PREPARING VEGETABLES FOR COOKING

Aubergine – Cut off the stalk and root and discard. Cut into 1cm/¹/₃in slices or chunks as you prefer.

Courgette – Cut off the stalk and root and discard. Cut into 1cm/¹/₃in slices or chunks as you prefer.

Fennel – Cut off the stalks from the top and the root from the bottom of the fennel bulb and discard. Cut the fennel bulb into slices or wedges as you wish.

Garlic – Lay the garlic cloves on their side on a chopping board and, using the side of your knife, push down on the clove taking care not to touch the knife's blade with your fingers. This will break the skin and make it easier to peel. Discard the skin. Cut off the end of the root at the bottom of the clove, then crush it in a garlic crusher.

Onion – Cut off the top and bottom of the onion and discard. Peel the onion and discard the skin. Cut the onion in half and slice as you wish.

Brunoise: fine dice of vegetables used for soups and as garnish

Paysanne: sliced shapes used for soups

Finely diced: small dice used during the cooking of dishes as a flavour enhancer

Turned: barrel-shaped vegetables and potatoes used for vegetable sides and garnishes

Julienne: fine strips of vegetables used for garnish

Tomato concasse: blanched, skinned and diced tomato flesh used for garnish

Small mirepoix: small dice used for making sauces, stews and braised dishes

Macedoine: medium diced squares used for large garnish

Large mirepoix: large diced vegetables used for stocks

BLANCHING

Prepared vegetables

Double the quantity of boiling, salted water

A large bowl of iced water

GET STUCK IN

1 Put your prepared vegetables, a batch at a time, in the boiling, salted water. It's important not to overfill the pan, otherwise the water temperature will drop too much.

2 Cook for as long as needed. Most vegetables only take a few minutes to blanch. For example, green beans will only take 2 minutes in boiling water. The best way to tell when it's ready is to take out a sample and try it, being careful not to burn yourself. Vegetables should have a slight bite.

3 Carefully remove the vegetables from the water, drain and refresh in the iced water. This will stop the cooking process and retain the colour and texture. Drain and keep chilled and covered until needed.

4 You can reheat in boiling, salted water or in the microwave. Also check the seasoning, and a little butter or olive oil can enhance the flavour.

BLANCHING: A TOMATO

STUFF YOU'LL NEED

Ripe tomatoes

Boiling water

Iced water

GET STUCK IN

1 Dig out the stalk on top of the tomato.

2 Criss-cross the other smooth end.

3 Blanch in rapidly boiling water for 12 seconds exactly. Immediately take out and plunge into iced water to stop the cooking process. This process makes the skin come away from the flesh then, using a small knife, you can peel the skin off.

ROASTING: SQUASH WITH THYME AND GARLIC

STUFF YOU'LL NEED

1 butternut squash

20ml/1½ tbsp olive oil

3 sprigs fresh thyme, leaves picked off

3 cloves garlic, finely chopped

Salt and freshly ground black pepper

20g/⅛ cup butter

GET STUCK IN

1 Preheat the oven to 200°C/400°F/gas 6.

2 Peel and cut the butternut squash into thick and even pieces. Place on an oiled roasting tray, drizzle with additional oil and sprinkle over the thyme leaves and chopped garlic. Season and mix together, evenly distributing the butter in small pieces.

3 Roast in the hot oven for 25–30 minutes or until the flesh is soft and golden brown. Turn every now and again during the cooking process.

MAKES 4 PORTIONS

Each portion contains:

Energy	Fat	Saturates	Sugars	Salt
804kJ 193kcals	9.4g	6.6g	7.0g	3.5g
10%	28%	33%	8%	58%

Of your reference intake

GRILLING: CAULIFLOWER CHEESE

STUFF YOU'LL NEED

1 cauliflower, cut into florets

20g/^{1}/$_8$ cup butter

Salt and freshly ground black pepper

250g/1 cup cheese sauce

70g/½ cup Cheddar cheese, grated

GET STUCK IN

1 Cook the cauliflower as per the blanching method (see page 94).

2 Reheat the cauliflower in a pan with the butter and season with salt and pepper.

3 Place the cauliflower in an ovenproof vegetable dish.

4 Coat with the cheese sauce and sprinkle over the grated Cheddar cheese.

5 Brown under a hot grill and serve.

MAKES 4 PORTIONS

Each portion contains:

Energy	Fat	Saturates	Sugars	Salt
1491kJ 355kcals	25.5g	15.5g	8.2g	1.3g
18%	36%	78%	9%	22%

Of your reference intake

BRAISING: RED CABBAGE

STUFF YOU'LL NEED

1 small red cabbage, quartered and finely shredded

Salt and freshly ground black pepper

100g/7 tbsp butter

1 cooking apple, peeled, cored and cut into 1cm/⅓in dice

2 star anise or 1 tsp ground cinnamon

40g/just under ¼ cup honey

200ml/¾ cup red wine vinegar

50g/¼ cup sultanas

GET STUCK IN

1 Preheat the oven to 180°C/350°F/gas 4.

2 Place the cabbage in a buttered casserole pot that has a tight-fitting lid and season with salt and pepper.

3 Add the butter, apple, star anise or cinnamon, honey, red wine vinegar and lastly the sultanas. Stir well.

4 Cover the cabbage with buttered parchment paper and place the lid on top. Cook in the oven for 1 hour without touching or stirring the pot.

5 Season to taste and serve.

MAKES 4 PORTIONS

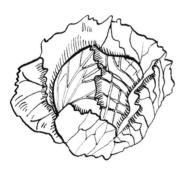

Each portion contains:

Energy	Fat	Saturates	Sugars	Salt
1247kJ 297kcals	21.1g	13.0g	22.3g	0.7g
15%	30%	65%	25%	12%

Of your reference intake

DEEP-FRYING: ONION RINGS

STUFF YOU'LL NEED

1 onion

100ml/7 tbsp milk

100g/¾ cup plain flour seasoned with salt and pepper

Sunflower oil, to deep-fry

Salt and freshly ground black pepper

GET STUCK IN

1 Peel the onion and cut it into 2mm slices in the round to produce big circles. Separate the rings.

2 Dip into the milk and then the seasoned flour, then do it again.

3 Half-fill a saucepan or deep-fat fryer (I would highly recommend using the latter as they are generally safer) with sunflower oil and heat the oil to about 180°C/350°F. Shake off any excess flour and deep-fry the onion rings in the hot oil until crisp and golden.

4 Using a slotted spoon, remove and drain on kitchen paper. Season with salt and pepper.

5 Serve immediately.

MAKES 4 PORTIONS

Note: Deep-fat frying can be dangerous if not done properly. Always remember the following:

• Use a large, wide, sturdy pan

• Make sure you have a close-fitting lid close to hand in case the oil catches fire

• Never put wet food in the fryer

• Never leave a pan of hot oil unattended; it can take just a minute or two for the oil to overheat and catch fire

• Turn off the fryer as soon as you have finished with it

Each portion contains:

Energy	Fat	Saturates	Sugars	Salt
602kJ 143kcals	2.8g	0.6g	4.4g	1.3g
7%	4%	3%	5%	21%

Of your reference intake

SHALLOW-FRYING: COURGETTES

STUFF YOU'LL NEED

2 courgettes

2 sprigs fresh rosemary

20ml/1½ tbsp olive oil

Salt and freshly ground
black pepper

GET STUCK IN

1 Wash, top and tail the courgette, then cut
into rounds 4cm/1½in thick.

2 Pick and chop the leaves from the
rosemary.

3 Heat the olive oil in a shallow frying pan,
carefully place the courgette rounds into
the pan, season with salt and pepper
and sprinkle with the chopped rosemary
leaves. Cook for 1 minute on each side,
take out of the pan and place on a piece
of kitchen paper to soak up the excess
oil. Transfer to a vegetable side dish
and serve.

MAKES 4 PORTIONS

Each portion contains:

Energy	Fat	Saturates	Sugars	Salt
346kJ	**5.9g**	**0.8g**	**2.9g**	**1.3g**
84kcals				
4%	8%	4%	3%	20%

Of your reference intake

STIR-FRYING: CHINESE VEGETABLES

STUFF YOU'LL NEED

100g/3½oz beansprouts

100g/3½oz shiitake
mushrooms

100g/3½oz carrots

100g/3½oz mangetout

50g/1¾oz red peppers

50g/1¾oz yellow peppers

100g/3½oz celery

50g/1¾oz baby sweetcorn

3 spring onions

10ml/2 tsp sunflower oil

10ml/2 tsp sesame oil

5g/¼oz piece of fresh root
ginger, peeled and finely
chopped

I clove garlic, crushed

10g/2 tsp honey

60ml/¼ cup soy sauce

Salt and freshly ground
black pepper

GET STUCK IN

1 Wash and trim all the vegetables: slice
the mushrooms, discarding the stalks;
julienne the carrots, mangetout, peppers,
celery and sweetcorn; and cut the
spring onions into fine rounds.

2 Heat a wok or high-sided frying pan
until it's very hot. Add the sunflower
and sesame oils to heat up. Add all the
vegetables and cook very quickly by
turning them over with some tongs. Try
not to remove the pan from the heat, as
this reduces the temperature too much.

3 After 3 minutes stir-frying, add the
ginger and garlic, and keep turning the
vegetables to mix them in. Drizzle over
the honey and soy sauce and turn the
vegetables again. Taste for seasoning
and serve immediately.

MAKES 4 PORTIONS

Each portion contains:

Energy	Fat	Saturates	Sugars	Salt
487kJ	5.5g	0.7g	8.8g	2.13g
114kcals				
6%	8%	4%	10%	36%

Of your reference intake

STEWING: RATATOUILLE

STUFF YOU'LL NEED

1 onion, sliced

1 fennel head, sliced

100ml/7 tbsp olive oil

3 cloves garlic, crushed

1 aubergine, cut into 1cm/^{1}/$_3$in rounds

1 red pepper, deseeded and sliced

1 yellow pepper, deseeded and sliced

2 courgettes, cut into 1cm/^{1}/$_3$in rounds

Salt and freshly ground black pepper

3 sprigs fresh thyme

1 x 400g/14oz tin chopped plum tomatoes

1 small handful of fresh parsley, chopped

Extra virgin olive oil

GET STUCK IN

1 Wash all the vegetables.

2 Top and tail as necessary, discarding any unwanted ends and seeds (see page 92 for instructions on preparing vegetables).

3 Cut into 1cm/1/3in dice or rounds, whichever you prefer.

4 In a large pan, fry the onion and fennel in the olive oil for 3–4 minutes without colouring, add the garlic and continue to cook for another couple of minutes.

5 Add the aubergine and peppers, turn the heat up a little and stir-fry for a further 3 minutes.

6 Add the courgettes, season with salt and pepper, and sprinkle over the thyme leaves. Stir-fry for another couple of minutes.

7 Add the chopped tomatoes and cover, then turn down the heat and cook for 10 minutes or until all the vegetables are tender. Take out and place into a vegetable side dish.

8 Sprinkle with the chopped parsley and a touch of extra virgin olive oil.

MAKES 4 PORTIONS

Each portion contains:

Energy	Fat	Saturates	Sugars	Salt
1316kJ	26.0g	3.8g	11.2g	1.27g
318kcals				
15%	37%	19%	12%	21%

Of your reference intake

POTATOES

Potatoes are amazing – probably one of the most versatile commodities grown in the world. Potatoes are tubers. They grow underground and can have different skin colours – white, brown, purple or red. The UK grows many varieties and is one of the world's biggest consumers of the potato.

When you buy potatoes, try not to buy the soft wrinkly ones. The skin should be firm and smooth. You don't want black bruises, big cracks or ones that generally look sorry for themselves. They shouldn't be sprouting either.

There are certain potatoes that do the job better than others. Here is is a rough guide to the two main kinds.

Floury potatoes

Floury potatoes are best for baking, mashing and chipping. They tend to break up if they are boiled. King Edward or Maris Piper.

Waxy potatoes

Waxy potatoes are a more solid, compact potato. They hold their shape and are more robust when boiled in water. But since they are waxy, they don't make good mashed potato. However, they are good for potato dishes such as boulangère and dauphinoise. Charlotte, or New.

And the following are best for:

Cara: boil or chip

Charlotte: boil or potato salad

Desirée: boil, roast, bake, mash or chip

King Edward: boil, bake, roast, mash or chip

Maris Piper: boil, roast, mash or chip

New: boil or roast

BOILED POTATOES

500g/1lb 2oz potatoes

Salt and freshly ground
black pepper

25g/⅛ cup butter, melted

1 handful of fresh parsley,
chopped

GET STUCK IN

1 Wash, peel and rewash the potatoes.

2 Cut or turn the potatoes into even sizes.

3 Cook carefully in lightly salted water
for 15 minutes or until the potatoes are
only just cooked through. To tell if they
are cooked, gently insert a sharp knife
into one and if it goes in easily they are
ready.

4 Carefully drain into a saucepan with
melted butter. Season and turn gently.
Serve into a vegetable dish and sprinkle
liberally with the chopped parsley.

MAKES 4 PORTIONS

Each portion contains:

Energy	Fat	Saturates	Sugars	Salt
588kJ 140kcals	5.4g	3.3g	0.8g	0.1g
7%	8%	16%	1%	2%

Of your reference intake

104

BAKED POTATOES IN THEIR JACKETS

STUFF YOU'LL NEED

1 medium to large potato per person

10ml/2 tsp olive oil

Salt

Butter, to serve

GET STUCK IN

1 When baking potatoes, don't just throw them in the oven. Take the time to prepare them properly and you'll be rewarded with a delicious, fluffy potato with a crispy skin.

2 Wash and scrub the potatoes. Preheat the oven to 220°C/425°F/gas 7.

3 Make diagonal 2mm deep incisions at 2cm/$^4/_5$in intervals around the potato with a sharp knife.

4 Drizzle with the olive oil and smooth it round each potato. Season all over with the salt.

5 Place on a rack and bake in the oven for 1–1½ hours.

6 Give the potatoes a little squeeze to check if they feel soft and cooked.

7 Take them out of the oven and cut a deep slit through the middle to let the steam out.

8 Serve immediately with some fresh, cold butter popped in the top.

Each portion contains:

Energy	Fat	Saturates	Sugars	Salt
625kJ 149kcals	5.5g	3.5g	1.3g	0.7g
7%	8%	18%	1%	12%

Of your reference intake

MASH

To make good mash, you need to understand the science behind the process. The starch in the potato absorbs the water and swells when cooking.

Then, when you mash the potato, the cells break down and more starch is released, which makes the potatoes creamy and smooth. When boiling, take your time and start from cold water. Bring to the boil, then drain and refresh in cold water and repeat the process. This time continue cooking until the potatoes are cooked through and a sharp knife slides in easily. This takes longer, but this extra step helps and, the longer it takes, the more starch will be released. It will allow the potatoes to absorb more liquid and butter.

Whenever you make mash, the first thing to put in it after draining the potatoes is the butter, as it coats the cells and prevents the mash from becoming gluey. Then add the warm milk and stir it well to lighten it.

MASH

STUFF YOU'LL NEED

500g/1lb 2oz floury
  potatoes

Salt and freshly ground
  black pepper

25g/^{1}/$_8$ cup butter

30ml/2 tbsp full-fat milk,
  warmed

2 spring onions, thinly
  sliced (optional)

GET STUCK IN

1 Wash, peel and rewash the potatoes,
  then cut into even-sized pieces.

2 Place in cold, salted water and bring to
  the boil.

3 Boil for 2–3 minutes.

4 Drain and repeat the process. This time
  continue cooking until the potatoes are
  cooked through and a sharp knife slides
  in easily.

5 Pass the potatoes through a potato ricer
  or use a simple potato masher. Do not
  use an electric blender, as you will only
  achieve a glue-like consistency.

6 Add the butter and whip together, slowly
  add the milk and continue to whip.
  Check for seasoning and serve.

Note: mash with spring onions gives an
interesting twist.

MAKES 4 PORTIONS

Each portion contains:

Energy	Fat	Saturates	Sugars	Salt
625kJ **149kcals**	**5.5g**	**3.5g**	**1.3g**	**0.7g**
7%	8%	18%	1%	12%

Of your reference intake

CHIPS

500g/1lb 2oz Russet potatoes

1.5 litres/6¼ cups groundnut oil

Plenty of salt

GET STUCK IN

1 Wash, peel and cut the potatoes into 1cm/⅓in x 5cm/2in-long chips.

2 Wash well and place in boiling, salted water for 8 minutes.

3 Remove and place on a drainer to cool. Place in the fridge until cold.

4 Half-fill a saucepan or deep-fat fryer with oil and heat up the oil to 160°C/320°F for 5–6 minutes or until lightly golden.

5 Remove with a slotted spoon and drain in a bowl lined with kitchen paper. Place on a tray and store until needed.

6 When you are ready to eat the chips, set the fryer at 180°C/350°F, put the chips into the basket and carefully place them into the hot fat, cooking until crisp and golden.

7 Drain well and place on kitchen paper. Season with salt and serve immediately.

MAKES 4 PORTIONS

Each portion contains:

Energy	Fat	Saturates	Sugars	Salt
1256kJ 299kcals	15.5g	2.0g	2.0g	0.1g
15%	22%	10%	2%	2%

Of your reference intake

BRAISED POTATOES

STUFF YOU'LL NEED

500g/1lb 2oz Russet potatoes

25ml/5 tsp olive oil

75g/$^1/_3$ cup butter

Salt

200ml/¾ cup good strong brown chicken stock (see page 60)

1 sprig fresh thyme

GET STUCK IN

1 Pick out some even-sized medium potatoes.

2 Wash, peel and rewash. Top and tail and cut in half.

3 Round off the edges from the cut sides.

4 Heat a pan and add the olive oil and one-third of the butter. Add the potatoes and sauté until the potatoes are coloured all over. Season with salt.

5 Place the potatoes on their flat sides.

6 Add the second third of the butter and heat to a foam.

7 Pour in the stock and bring to the boil, add the thyme and place in the oven.

8 Baste from time to time, making sure the potatoes are not sticking to the pan base.

9 They will be cooked when a knife can go through them with little effort and the stock will be absorbed.

10 Add the remaining butter and baste well, then reserve the potatoes until needed.

MAKES 4 PORTIONS

Each portion contains:

Energy	Fat	Saturates	Sugars	Salt
995kJ 237kcals	16.0g	9.8g	0.8g	0.8g
12%	23%	49%	1%	13%

Of your reference intake

PERFECT ROASTIES

STUFF YOU'LL NEED

1kg/2lb 4oz
Maris Piper
potatoes

Salt

100ml/7 tbsp
olive oil

2 tsp plain
flour

GET STUCK IN

1 Put a roasting tin in the oven (one big enough to take the potatoes in a single layer) and preheat the oven to 200°C/400°F/gas 6. Peel the potatoes and cut each into 4 even-sized pieces if the potatoes are medium size, 2–3 pieces if smaller. Drop the potatoes into a large pan and pour in enough water so that they are just covered. Add salt, then wait for the water to boil. As soon as the water reaches a full rolling boil, lower the heat, put your timer on and simmer the potatoes uncovered, reasonably vigorously, for 2 minutes. Meanwhile, put the oil in the hot roasting tin and heat it in the oven for a few minutes so it's really hot.

2 Drain the potatoes in a colander. Now it's time to rough them up a bit – shake the colander back and forth a few times to fluff up the outsides. Sprinkle with the flour, and give another shake or two so they are evenly and thinly coated. Carefully put the potatoes in the hot fat – they will sizzle as they go in – then turn and roll them around so they are coated all over. Spread them in a single layer, making sure they have plenty of room.

3 Roast the potatoes for 15 minutes in the hot oven, then take them out and turn them over. Roast for another 15 minutes then turn them over again. Put them back in the oven for another 10–20 minutes, or however long it takes to get them really golden and crisp. The colouring will be uneven, which is what you want. Scatter with salt and serve straightaway.

Each portion contains:

Energy	Fat	Saturates	Sugars	Salt
1256kJ 299kcals	15.5g	2.0g	2.0g	0.1g
15%	22%	10%	2%	2%

Of your reference intake

POULTRY

Poultry is a term for domestic fowl and includes chicken, turkey, duck, goose and pigeon. I'm going to concentrate on chicken, as it's by far the most popular, but you can apply most of what I say to all other birds.

Obviously, the size of each chicken is different, which means that cooking times will vary as a result. All birds have similar bodies, however, so the method of cutting them up will be exactly the same.

CHICKEN

You can buy various types of chicken in a supermarket. Here's a rough guide:

Basic supermarket range – This is usually the cheapest chicken available. The chickens have been raised in purpose-built buildings eating various grains.

Corn-fed – The chickens have had a diet with a high corn content, giving the meat a yellowish colour.

Free-range – The chickens have been able to roam freely on farmland, where they've been able to forage for their food during the day. Closer to the way chickens would naturally behave, free-range chicken is said to be a more ethical food.

Organic – The chickens have only eaten an organic diet, with the grains uncontaminated by chemical pesticides and other chemicals.

In addition to whole chickens, you can also buy different cuts. Chicken breast is the most popular and the most expensive, as it has no bone and minimal fat. Thighs are a good alternative as they can come with or without bones and are meaty but with a bit more fat. Then there are the drumsticks. Cooking chicken pieces with the bones kept in can help the meat taste more succulent.

Buy the best-quality chicken you can afford and to suit your taste. I prefer to spend more on chicken but eat it less frequently so it becomes affordable.

Baby chicken

300–500g/11oz–1lb 3oz

1 portion

Small roasting chicken

750–1kg/1lb 10oz–2lb 2oz

2 portions

Medium roasting chicken

1–2kg/2lb 2oz–4lb 4oz

4 portions

Large roasting chicken

2–3kg/4lb 4oz–6lb 6oz

6 portions

Capon

3–4.5kg/6lb 6oz–9lb 9oz

8 portions

Old boiling fowl (for soup)

2.5–4kg/5lb 5oz–8lb 8oz

Chickens contain approximately 20 per cent bone, so they're lean and full of protein. This means they are good for our bodies, helping us to build and repair body tissues and providing energy.

They should be stored at a chilled temperature or frozen. Chicken naturally contains salmonella, so care should be taken not to cross-contaminate with other foods, in particular ready-to-eat food.

When cooking chicken, make sure it is thawed out, doesn't smell off and is cooked through. Chicken should be plump and the flesh should be firm.

I never understand why people buy pieces of chicken. Buy the whole bird and cut it up. You get much more value for your money. It will usually provide you with at least two meals and you can make a stock from the bones that can be used for a soup or a risotto. It can be the most economical food available.

It is recommended that you don't wash the bird before cutting it up, as this will spread the bacteria all over your sink.

CUTTING UP A CHICKEN

Chicken can be cut up into 10–12 useable pieces.

Don't forget, all birds have the same bodies, so if you learn to do this with a chicken, you will be able to cut up any bird.

- Remove the wingettes – these are my favourite part of the chicken, either roasted crisp on the chicken or bought in a packet and marinated before roasted or deep-fried, and are always packed with flavour
- Remove the legs from the carcass, cutting around the oyster on each side (the oyster is a piece of dark meat sitting in a dip by the thighs)
- Most chicken bought from the supermarket comes without feet, but cut off the feet if this hasn't yet been done
- Separate the thigh from the drumstick
- Trim the drumstick by cutting off the knuckle
- Remove each breast from the carcass
- Separate the wing from the breasts and trim it
- Cut into the cavity, splitting the carcass (use the carcass for stock)
- Cut each breast in half

BRAISED CHICKEN LEGS WITH MUSHROOMS

STUFF YOU'LL NEED

4 chicken legs (4 drumsticks & 4 thighs)

Salt and freshly ground black pepper

1 tbsp olive oil

1 onion, chopped

2 cloves garlic, chopped

2 rashers smoked bacon, sliced

100g/3½oz chestnut mushrooms, sliced

50g/1¾oz dried wild mushrooms, soaked twice in warm water and drained, sliced

1 tbsp plain flour

1 tbsp tomato purée

1 glass red wine (optional)

200ml/¾ cup brown chicken stock (see page 60)

2 tomatoes, chopped

1 handful of fresh parsley or tarragon, chopped

GET STUCK IN

1 Season the chicken with salt and pepper. Heat the olive oil in a pan and pan-fry the chicken, try to get a nice colour on each side. Take out each piece of chicken and reserve on a plate.

2 Add the onion, garlic and bacon to the pan and keep it all moving.

3 Once the onion is softening and the bacon is colouring, add in the raw and soaked mushrooms, mix well and continue cooking for 3–4 minutes.

4 Return the chicken to the pan. Sprinkle the flour over and turn the chicken in order to coat each piece. Add the tomato purée and mix in.

5 Pour in the wine (if using) and bring to the boil.

6 Pour in the stock and bring to the boil once again, then turn down to a simmer. Place a lid on the pan and cook very gently for an hour. Check regularly that the base of the pan is not sticking.

Each portion contains:

Energy	Fat	Saturates	Sugars	Salt
1016kJ 242kcals	11.5g	2.9g	4.1g	1.1g
12%	16%	14%	5%	18%

Of your reference intake

7 Once the chicken is cooked through nicely, take out each piece and place in a serving dish. Add the tomatoes and check the seasoning.

8 Pour the sauce over the chicken pieces, sprinkle with the chopped herbs and serve.

MAKES 4 PORTIONS

GRILLED CHICKEN

STUFF YOU'LL NEED

4 legs or 8 pieces of chicken

Salt and freshly ground black pepper

1 tbsp olive oil or 20g/ ¹/₈ cup butter

1 lemon

GET STUCK IN

1 Season the chicken with salt and pepper.

2 Brush with olive oil or melted butter and place on a greased tray.

3 Place under the grill or on top of a barbecue.

4 Brush frequently with the fat as it melts onto the tray. Allow approximately 15–20 minutes depending on the thickness of the pieces of chicken.

5 Make sure it's cooked through. Test by cutting a drumstick to the bone to see if it's cooked and there's no blood.

6 Squeeze on lemon juice and serve with a salad and chips (see page 108).

MAKES 4 PORTIONS

Each portion contains:

Energy	Fat	Saturates	Sugars	Salt
1550kJ	**27.0g**	**6.7g**	**0.9g**	**1.0g**
369kcals				
18%	39%	34%	0%	17%

Of your reference intake

ROAST CHICKEN

STUFF YOU'LL NEED

1 x 1.5kg/3lb 5oz chicken

Salt and freshly ground black pepper

1 lemon

1 head garlic

1 bunch fresh thyme

2 tbsp extra virgin olive oil

20g/¹/₈ cup butter

50ml/¼ cup white wine

200ml/¾ cup brown chicken stock (see page 60)

GET STUCK IN

1 Preheat the oven to 220°C/425°F/gas 7.

2 Place the chicken onto a roasting tray and season well on both sides.

3 Slice the lemon, squash the garlic and pick the thyme, then use these to marinate the chicken, massaging it all over. Drizzle over the olive oil, smear on the butter and season well.

4 Place the chicken in the oven and turn it down to 200°C/400°F/gas 6. Baste regularly. The chicken should take about 1–1½ hours to cook.

5 Once the chicken is cooked, clear juices should appear from the leg if a small knife is inserted.

6 Take it out of the oven and rest for at least 30 minutes. This way the chicken will stay juicy and the meat will just fall off the bone. Carefully pour out the fat from the tray and pour in the white wine and stock. Reduce to the required sauce consistency and season to taste.

7 Strain into a jug.

8 Reheat the chicken by adding a ladle of gravy to the bottom of the dish, baste

Each portion contains:

Energy	Fat	Saturates	Sugars	Salt
2122kJ 504kcals	14.1g	4.6g	0.5g	1.4g
25%	20%	23%	1%	23%

Of your reference intake

with reserved chicken fat and cover with tin foil.
Place in the oven at 120°C/250°F/gas 1 for 10–15
minutes or until the meat is hot all the way through.

9 Serve with roast potatoes (see page 110) and
vegetables.

MAKES 4 PORTIONS

SWEET AND SOUR CHICKEN

STUFF YOU'LL NEED

1 x 425g/15oz tin pineapple
chunks in natural juice

2 tbsp cornflour

150ml/⅔ cup water

2 tbsp dark soy sauce

2 tbsp white wine vinegar

2 tbsp soft light brown sugar

2 tbsp tomato ketchup

1 tsp dried chilli flakes

2 skinless, boneless chicken
breasts

2 tbsp sunflower oil

1 medium onion, cut into 12
wedges

2 peppers, red, green, orange
or yellow, deseeded and
cut into chunks of about
3cm/1¼in

1 x 225g/8oz tin water
chestnuts

2 cloves garlic, crushed

25g/1oz piece of fresh root
ginger, peeled and finely
grated

Freshly ground black pepper

GET STUCK IN

1 To make the sauce, drain the
pineapple in a sieve over a bowl
and keep all the juice – you should
have about 150ml/²/₃ cup. Put the
cornflour in a large bowl and stir
in 3 tablespoons of the pineapple
juice to make a smooth paste. Add
the remaining juice and the water,
then stir in the soy sauce, vinegar,
sugar, ketchup and chilli flakes until
thoroughly combined. Set aside.

2 Cut each chicken breast into eight or
nine even pieces. Heat a tablespoon of
the oil in a large non-stick frying pan or
wok and stir-fry the onion and peppers
for 2 minutes over a high heat.

3 Drain the water chestnuts and cut them
in half horizontally.

4 Add the remaining oil and the chicken
to the pan and stir-fry for 2 minutes until
coloured on all sides. Add the garlic,
ginger, pineapple chunks and water
chestnuts and stir-fry for 30–60 seconds.

continued overleaf

5 Give the cornflour and pineapple mixture a good stir and add it to the pan with the chicken and vegetables. Stir well, season with some pepper and bring to a simmer.

6 Cook for 4–6 minutes until the sauce is thickened and glossy and the chicken is tender and cooked throughout, turning the chicken and vegetables a few times.

7 Serve with a small portion of rice (see page 79).

MAKES 4 PORTIONS

Each portion contains:

Energy	Fat	Saturates	Sugars	Salt
1294kJ	6.7g	0.9g	27.5g	1.4g
308kcals				
15%	10%	4%	31%	23%

Of your reference intake

LEMON AND PARMESAN CHICKEN

4 skinless, boneless chicken breasts

Zest of 1 lemon

1 clove garlic, chopped

Few sprigs fresh rosemary

2–3 tbsp olive oil

2 tbsp plain flour, for dipping

2 eggs, beaten

100g/1¼ cups Parmesan cheese, finely grated

4 slices white bread, made into crumbs

2–3 tbsp olive oil

375g/13¼oz uncooked dry weight penne pasta

200ml/¾ cup rich tomato sauce (see page 150)

1 bunch of fresh basil

GET STUCK IN

1 Cut the chicken breasts in half lengthways and marinate for 3 hours or overnight with the lemon zest, chopped garlic, rosemary and olive oil.

2 Preheat the oven to 200°C/400°F/gas 6.

3 Remove most of the marinade with a brush or cloth, then place the chicken in the flour, then in the eggs, then into the Parmesan.

4 Put the chicken back into the flour, followed by the eggs, then into the breadcrumbs. It is best to do this one at a time to avoid mess!

5 Heat the olive oil in a frying pan and gently fry the now-breaded chicken until golden, then place on an oven tray, transferring to the oven for 10 minutes until fully cooked.

6 Cook the pasta (see pages 76–7) and add the sauce. Heat through.

7 Take a warm serving bowl, put the pasta on the bottom and arrange the chicken on top, then pick off the basil leaves and sprinkle on top.

8 Serve with a nice green salad.

MAKES 4 PORTIONS

Each portion contains:

Energy	Fat	Saturates	Sugars	Salt
3475kJ 830kcals	39.5g	15.7g	5.0g	3.2g
42%	56%	78%	6%	54%

Of your reference intake

CHICKEN CURRY WITH SAFFRON AND ALMONDS

STUFF YOU'LL NEED

1.5kg/3lb 5oz chicken pieces, skin removed (2 legs; 2 breasts)

125ml/½ cup natural yoghurt

15g/½ oz piece of fresh root ginger, peeled and finely chopped

1 small onion, quartered

3 cloves garlic, crushed

2–3 dried chillies

1 onion, sliced

20g/$^1/_8$ cup butter

2 tsp garam masala

1 tsp black cumin seeds

2 green cardamom pods, husks removed and seeds crushed

1 tsp ground coriander

100ml/7 tbsp water

1 whole green chilli, chopped

1 tsp saffron strands

60ml/¼ cup coconut milk

150ml/$^2/_3$ cup double cream

Salt

6g/¼oz ground almonds

1 tbsp chopped coriander

1 lemon, juice and zest

GET STUCK IN

1 Cut each chicken joint in half, separating leg from thigh and cutting each breast into two pieces.

2 Mix the yoghurt and chopped ginger together with the chicken and cover. Leave to marinate for 2–4 hours or overnight in the fridge.

3 Place the quartered onion, garlic and dried chillies in a food processor/ liquidiser, blend until smooth – you may need a little water.

4 Fry the sliced onion in half the butter until golden brown.

5 When the sliced onions are brown, take them out, leaving the butter in the pan and reserve.

6 Add the rest of the butter and when hot add the garam masala, cumin seeds, cardamom seeds and ground coriander. Take off the heat if too hot.

7 Add the chicken and marinade juices. Adjust the heat to medium and cook for 10 minutes, stirring frequently.

8 Add the liquidised onion and continue cooking for 6 minutes.

9 Add the water, chilli, saffron, coconut milk, cream and fried onions and season with salt.

10 Turn the heat to low, cover the pan and simmer until the chicken is tender (25–30 minutes).

11 Sprinkle with the almonds and coriander and add the lemon juice and zest. Serve with some pilau rice (see page 80).

MAKES 4 PORTIONS

Each portion contains:

Energy	Fat	Saturates	Sugars	Salt
3383kJ **816kcals**	**62.7g**	**26.5g**	**9.5g**	**0.7g**
41%	**90%**	**132%**	**10%**	**12%**

Of your reference intake

FISH

Fish is one of the most interesting food products. It is ultra-good for you as it contains the best proteins, very little fat, and the fat it does contain is excellent for our bodies.

Fish can be split into two groups – flat and round – and then split again into oily fish and white fish.

Oily round fish include: mackerel, tuna, herring, salmon and sardines

Oily fish contains good fats and vitamins, as well as omega 3 and 6 oils, which are excellent for your brain, heart and circulation.

White round fish include: cod, whiting and hake

Flat white fish include: plaice, sole and turbot

White fish does not contain fat, and vitamins are only present in their livers. The bones do contain calcium but are rarely eaten.

There are tons of different fish, but overfishing means we need to be careful and the authorities are watching fish stocks. It's always best to buy fish off the boat if you're lucky enough to be able to; a fish market/shop is the next best thing. Supermarkets have obviously made it easier for us to buy prepared fish, but it's usually more expensive.

FISH QUALITY
When you buy fish, you need to be sure that it's fresh and good quality. Here are some things to look out for:

Whole

Clear, bright eyes, not sunken and clouded

Bright red gills

Scales intact

Moist skin, not slippery and slimy

Stiff tail and firm flesh

Fresh smell

Fillets

Neat and trim, firm flesh

Packed closely together

White and translucent colour, or a flush pink in the case of salmon fillets

Smoked

Glossy appearance

Firm flesh and not sticky

Nice smoked smell

Fish can be economical and isn't difficult to cook. If it's overcooked, it's not so pleasant to eat and, for me, represents a waste of money. Light cooking with simple flavours is the best way to eat this amazing food.

You should store fish in the fridge, in separate containers to avoid cross-contamination, especially from meat and poultry.

Fish has been eaten for so long we have also become good at preserving it by freezing, canning, salting, pickling and smoking. Personally, I don't think it freezes so well, but it is possible and keeping it dry and well wrapped makes it a better product to cook if you do decide to freeze it. Also, always make sure it's completely thawed out before cooking. Read the packaging to check if it has been frozen before; if so, don't refreeze it.

PREPARING FISH

Usually we use about 100–120g/3½–4¼oz per portion when it's served off the bone; an extra third should be accounted for when buying whole fish. All fish should be washed under cold running water before and after preparation. Whole fish should have their fins trimmed, scales removed and guts and gills cut out before they are rewashed.

Gutting and scaling:

Do so from the vent to two-thirds along the fish belly.

Draw out the intestines with your fingers. Wash thoroughly. Ensure any blood lying along the bone is removed.

Using a scaler or palette knife, remove the scales by skimming the skin surface in the opposite direction to the scales' natural direction; keep repeating the strokes to remove them all, using your fingers to feel for remaining scales.

HOW TO TELL IF FISH IS COOKED

Cooked fish is white and flaky. To check the fish is cooked, put a fork into the thickest section of the fish. Twist the fork to see if the flesh breaks away easily. If it does, the fish is done. If there is some resistance, the fish is still raw inside, so cook it for a little longer.

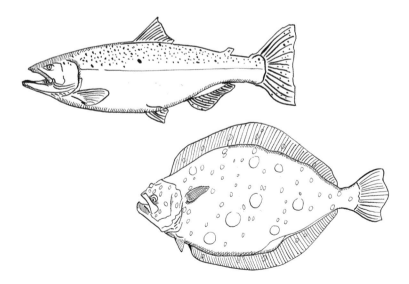

CURED SALMON WITH SOY LEMON DRESSING

STUFF YOU'LL NEED

Salt and freshly ground white pepper

350g/12½oz extremely fresh salmon fillet

3 sprigs fresh coriander

12 thin slices pickled ginger

For the soy lemon dressing

2 tbsp lemon juice

1 tbsp light soy sauce

1 tsp honey

1 tbsp sesame oil

3 tbsp extra virgin olive oil

1 small red chilli, finely chopped

GET STUCK IN

1 Season the plates lightly with salt and pepper to taste.

2 Cut the salmon into very fine slices and arrange in a circle on each dressed plate.

3 To make the lemon dressing, place all the ingredients into a blender and whizz until smooth, then strain.

4 Half an hour before serving, drizzle the dressing over the salmon, ensuring all the fish is covered. It is best to use a plastic sauce bottle.

5 Place approximately 3 sprigs of coriander and slices of pickled ginger evenly around the fish.

MAKES 4 PORTIONS

Each portion contains:

Energy	Fat	Saturates	Sugars	Salt
1398kJ 337kcals	27.3g	4.2g	3.9g	1.1g
17%	39%	21%	4%	18%

Of your reference intake

BAKED COD WITH PARSLEY CRUST

STUFF YOU'LL NEED

20g/¾oz onion, finely chopped

1 clove garlic, finely chopped

75g/¹/₃ cup butter, plus a little extra

100g/3½oz fresh white breadcrumbs

1 lemon, zest and juice

1 handful of fresh parsley, finely chopped

olive oil (optional)

Salt and freshly ground black pepper

4 x 150g/5¼oz cod fillets

GET STUCK IN

1 Preheat the oven to 180°C/350°F/gas 4.

2 Sweat the onion and garlic in the butter until soft and transparent; don't allow to colour. Place on a plate and cool.

3 Put the breadcrumbs, lemon zest and parsley in a food processor and switch on. Blitz until it's nice and green, add a little olive oil if necessary.

4 Mix the onion with the green breadcrumbs, then season with salt and pepper.

5 Season the cod fillet with salt and black pepper and coat thinly with the little extra butter. Cook in the oven for about 4 minutes.

6 Remove from the oven and sprinkle a heavy layer of the onion and breadcrumb crust onto the cod before placing back in the oven for a further 2 minutes.

7 Heat the lemon juice and gradually add the garlic butter until emulsified. Pour around the outside of the plate. Place on a serving plate and serve with mash potatoes with spring onions (see page 107).

MAKES 4 PORTIONS

Each portion contains:

Energy	Fat	Saturates	Sugars	Salt
1407kJ 335kcals	15.9g	9.3g	1.3g	1.2g
17%	23%	47%	1%	20%

Of your reference intake

PAN-FRIED MACKEREL WITH POMEGRANATE AND HONEY DRESSING

STUFF YOU'LL NEED

2 tbsp extra virgin olive oil

4 fresh mackerel fillets, pin-boned and cut into two equal pieces

Salt and freshly ground black pepper

1 large bunch of wild rocket, washed

1 cucumber, peeled and sliced

100g/4oz cherry tomatoes, halved

For the dressing

1 tsp salt

1 pomegranate, seeded

2 tsp honey

1 small shallot, finely chopped

1 tsp grain mustard

1 level tsp capers, finely chopped

1 red pepper, deseeded and diced fairly small

1 large bunch of fresh mint, finely chopped

1 tsp red wine vinegar

4 tbsp extra virgin olive oil

Pinch of dried chilli flakes

Salt and freshly ground black pepper

GET STUCK IN

1 Mix all the dressing ingredients into a bowl, season, combine thoroughly and reserve.

2 Heat a frying pan until hot. Add the olive oil.

3 Season the mackerel fillets and then place skin-side down in the hot frying pan. Cook for 3 minutes and then turn and cook for a further 3 minutes on the other side. Remove the fish from the pan and place on a tray.

4 To serve, place the rocket, cucumber and cherry tomatoes in a large bowl. Mix up the dressing and drizzle 4 or 5 tablespoons over the salad, mixing it around the bowl.

5 Take a small handful of salad and place in the middle of each plate.

Each portion contains:

Energy 2579kJ 622kcals	Fat 48.4g	Saturates 9.9g	Sugars 8.9g	Salt 1.7g
31%	69%	50%	10%	28%

Of your reference intake

6 Using a fish slice, place two warm mackerel fillets on each plate.

7 Spoon the remaining dressing around and serve immediately.

MAKES 4 PORTIONS

POACHED SALMON

STUFF YOU'LL NEED

1 carrot, thinly sliced

1 onion, thinly sliced

3 lemon, slices

500ml/2 cups water

Salt and freshly ground black pepper

4 x 150g/5¼oz salmon fillets

GET STUCK IN

1 Place the carrot, onion and lemon in the water and bring to the boil. Season to taste.

2 Place the prepared salmon fillets into the simmering water and turn off. Leave for 5 minutes.

3 Take out the salmon, pat dry and serve with new potatoes, salad and mayonnaise.

MAKES 4 PORTIONS

Each portion contains:

Energy 924kJ 220kcals	Fat 13.0g	Saturates 2.3g	Sugars 1.2g	Salt 0.7g
11%	19%	11%	1%	12%

Of your reference intake

GRILLED FILLETS OF SOLE

STUFF YOU'LL NEED

4 fillets of sole

Olive oil

Salt and freshly ground
black pepper

1 lemon

GET STUCK IN

1 Ensure the fish is clean and pat dry.

2 Score the fillets lightly on the skin side
two or three times to stop the fish from
curling up when it cooks.

3 Brush with olive oil and season with salt
and pepper.

4 Place under a hot grill for 3-4 minutes
depending on thickness.

5 Once the fish is cooked (see page 127),
remove from the grill, squeeze the lemon
over it and serve on a plate, drizzled with
the tray juices.

6 Serve with a simple dressed salad.

MAKES 4 PORTIONS

Each portion contains:

Energy	Fat	Saturates	Sugars	Salt
218kJ **52kcals**	**1.1g**	**0.2g**	**0.1g**	**0.3g**
3%	2%	1%	0%	5%

Of your reference intake

MEAT

I find meat a fascinating subject. It's quite controversial for some people - vegetarians and vegans, for example - who won't eat it, as they believe that killing animals is wrong, while others reject it for health or environmental reasons. Some religions forbid their followers to eat certain animals or require the animals to be killed in a certain way. Then there's the issue of how the animals are reared. Some methods are unpopular, but ensure that the meat is more affordable. People are now becoming concerned about what the animals themselves have eaten and where the meat has been produced.

Whatever your beliefs, there are some basic facts about meat that need to be understood in order to prepare and cook it successfully.

In the main, meat is selected by breed. All animals are given specially produced feed that will enable them to grow a certain way. Today, we like leaner animals that have a better ratio of flesh to fat. In years gone by, we preferred more fat. As our diets have changed, so has the meat we produce. Meat is basically lots of fibre that is bound by connective tissue. During butchery, most of the connective tissue is removed, as cooking cannot make it soft enough to eat. However, some tougher, fibrous cuts can be cooked slowly and are very delicious, especially meat from older animals, but good cooking skills are needed.

Fat is a good thing in meat. Generally, the butcher will leave fat on the meat where it can help with flavour and aid moistness when being cooked as a roast joint, for example. Fat quantities vary in the different animals and even in the various breeds of the same animal. Fat is on the outside of the animal and it also runs through the meat. We call this marbling and it can be seen as a sign of quality. After an animal is killed, it is hung. This is important for tenderness – the longer it's hung, the more tender it becomes. The process usually takes around one to three weeks, depending on the animal.

PRESERVING MEAT

As with fish, over the years we have learned to preserve meat in different ways in order to keep it longer and get the most out of it. These methods include chilling, freezing, canning, salting and smoking.

PROPER STORAGE AND PREPARATION OF MEAT

All meat should be stored in the fridge or freezer.

It should be wrapped up well to avoid any juices or blood escaping. Label and date it so that you know it's going to be safe to eat.

When you prepare any meat, care needs to be taken not to cross-contaminate the raw meat with your kitchen equipment, other parts of the kitchen and especially ready-to-eat food. So it's a good idea to clear sufficient space, and always clean all the surfaces before and after you have prepared the meat, using hot soapy water and sanitiser.

It goes without saying that you should buy meat from a reputable retailer. A butcher, market or supermarket is best. Someone's car boot is not the place from which to buy meat and could be dangerous.

Meat is not always a uniform product, so different animals will have different sizes of cuts and the meat and fat may differ in colour. Very red meat is freshly cut. As the hours tick by after cutting, it darkens and will eventually turn brown. This doesn't necessarily mean it's not good to eat. I like to marinate meat as soon as I get it. Rubbing it with a little olive oil prevents the oxygen from discolouring the meat quite as fast.

CHOOSING AND BUYING MEAT

What cut to buy and cook is made simpler if you think about what that cut might have done when the animal was alive. Most cuts from the back end of the animal are tender, whereas those from the forward end are tougher, requiring longer and slower cooking. This is because animals use their front ends to do most of the work. They are especially tough around the neck, as they need to move their heavy heads up and down to feed. Therefore, the muscles are particularly strong here.

COOKING MEAT

Meat is a fantastic product, as it's so versatile. Eating it raw is tricky, as it is mostly muscle tissue. Cutting it thinly and curing it, or mincing it for beef tartare, is really the only way to eat it raw.

Cooking meat changes its texture entirely and enables you to eat it. Tougher cuts need longer, slower cooking, often in liquids. During cooking, the tenderising process takes place, softening the tissues.

Cooking also renders down unnecessary fats, allowing the flavours to come out and penetrate the meat positively. Searing or frying meat is a good thing, as it helps break down the fat whilst the colouring process also brings that lovely meaty, caramelised, savoury flavour we all love so much. Meat with little colour can look unappetising, which you don't want for larger cuts. As they relax, the juices seep back in and the meat moistens and becomes more tender. Basting is important at this stage to make sure the juices aren't lost.

Meat cooked on the bone gains flavour and tends to be more moist once carved. Meat bones can be used for stocks and are very flavourful. They should not be thrown away if at all possible. Get the most out of what you buy.

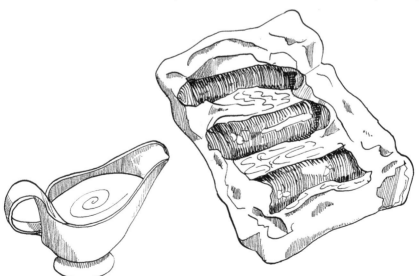

COOKING TEMPERATURES OF MEAT

It's a good idea to use a cooking thermometer when cooking meat. Here is a simple guide to core temperatures that meat should reach during cooking:

BEEF	rare 52°C/125°F medium 57°C/134°F well done 62°C/143°F
LAMB	pink 57°C/134°F well done 62°C/143°F
PORK	57°C/134°F
VEAL	62°C/143°F
CHICKEN, TURKEY	77°C/170°F
DUCK	pink 57°C/134°F well done 62°C/143°F

QUALITY

Most animals have their own quality points, but in general meat from smaller animals such as lamb and pork should have white fat and not too much around the flesh. Beef fat tends to be more yellow.

Meat should be fairly firm and have a nice texture to it. Different animals have different colours. The best way to learn what you're looking for is to head down to a good butcher or market and ask to be shown all their products. They will be more than happy to help if it's not a busy time.

Briefly, in its raw state veal and pork are pale pink, lamb is bright red, mutton should be a darker red and beef varies from fresh red to dark red, depending on when it was cut and how long it's been hung for.

Many people like animal offal, and this stems from years of making sure we that we eat every last bit of the animal. I'm in favour of this to avoid waste. But not everyone likes offal, so always check before cooking it for someone.

MUTTON SHEPHERD'S PIE

STUFF YOU'LL NEED

2 tbsp olive oil

1kg/2lb 4oz shoulder of mutton or lamb

Salt and freshly ground black pepper

2 onions, finely chopped

4 sprigs fresh thyme, chopped

4 cloves garlic, chopped

60g/¼ cup butter

2 tbsp tomato purée

2 tbsp plain flour

1 glass red wine

2 tbsp Worcestershire sauce

1 litre/4¼ cups brown chicken stock (see page 60)

Mashed potato (see page 107)

75g/⅔ cup Cheddar cheese, grated

GET STUCK IN

1 In a large frying pan, heat the olive oil until hot, add the mutton, season with black pepper and fry until well browned on all sides. Remove the meat from the pan and place in a roasting tray.

2 Add the onions to the pan with the thyme and garlic and a knob of butter, and cook until soft and translucent. Add the tomato purée, then sprinkle over the flour. Cook, stirring constantly, for 2–3 minutes to incorporate the flour.

3 Add the red wine, Worcestershire sauce, chicken stock and salt and pepper and bring back to a simmer and add all of this into the roasting pan with the mutton.

4 Braise this for at least 2 hours at 160°C/320°F/gas 3, maybe longer, until the meat is flaking from the bone. At this point, remove the shoulder from the liquid and leave to become cool enough to handle. Should the gravy require further thickening, reduce on the heat as required.

5 Flake the meat and add back into the gravy, while reserving any of the gravy you can to serve, then cool until ready to assemble. Reserve the bone and trimmings for stock.

Each portion contains:

Energy	Fat	Saturates	Sugars	Salt
4261kJ 1025kcals	71.1g	34.3g	7.8g	3.9g
51%	102%	171%	9%	66%

Of your reference intake

6 Spoon the meat and cooking liquid into a casserole and cover with mashed potato. Fluff it up with the back of a fork. Sprinkle with the grated cheese.

7 Bake at 190°C/375°F/gas 5 for 25–35 minutes until golden brown. Serve immediately.

MAKES 4 PORTIONS

GRILLED LAMB CHOPS

STUFF YOU'LL NEED

2 lamb chops per person

Salt and freshly ground black pepper

Sprigs fresh rosemary, chopped

Olive oil

Juice of ½ lemon

GET STUCK IN

1 Season the chops with salt, pepper and the chopped rosemary sprigs.

2 Rub the chops with olive oil and place on a greased tray.

3 Place under a hot grill or onto a hot barbecue.

4 Cook for 2–3 minutes, turn over and do the same again. This seals the pores and stops the unnecessary leaking of lovely juices. Cook for a further 3–4 minutes on each side.

5 Take out from under the grill and squeeze over a little lemon juice

6 Serve with chips (see page 108) and a nice fresh salad.

Each portion contains:

Energy 1659kJ 399kcals	Fat 28.8g	Saturates 13.7g	Sugars 0.2g	Salt 0.5g
20%	41%	68%	0%	8%

Of your reference intake

SPAGHETTI BOLOGNESE

STUFF YOU'LL NEED

2 tbsp olive oil and extra to serve

10 slices pancetta, sliced

1 tbsp chopped rosemary

3 cloves garlic, finely chopped

1 large onion, finely diced

450g/1lb best-quality minced beef

1 glass red wine

2 x 400g/14oz tins plum tomatoes

1 tbsp fresh oregano

200ml/¾ cup tomato purée

Sea salt and freshly ground black pepper

500g/1lb 2oz dried spaghetti

1 handful of fresh basil, torn

2 tbsp freshly grated Parmesan cheese

GET STUCK IN

1 Preheat the oven to 180°C/350°F/gas 4.

2 Place a large non-stick pan on the heat. Add the olive oil, pancetta and rosemary and cook until lightly golden, then add the garlic and onion.

3 Sauté for a further 3 minutes.

4 Add the minced beef, making sure it is browned all over, then add the red wine and reduce by a quarter. Now add the tomatoes, remembering to crush them slightly with your spoon. Add the oregano and tomato purée.

5 Season and bring to the boil, then cover and place in the oven for 1½ hours.

6 Towards the end of cooking, place the pasta in a pot of boiling, salted water and mix the torn basil through the Bolognese sauce.

7 Once the pasta is cooked, drain well, keeping a bit of the water to toss the pasta in before serving so it doesn't dry out.

8 Serve the pasta first and spoon the Bolognese on top, followed by the Parmesan and a drizzle of olive oil.

MAKES 4 PORTIONS

Each portion contains:

Energy	Fat	Saturates	Sugars	Salt
4217kJ 1004kcals	38.4g	13.7g	19.3g	03.9g
50%	55%	68%	21%	65%

Of your reference intake

BAKED TOAD IN THE HOLE

STUFF YOU'LL NEED

130g/1 cup plain flour

1 tsp salt

2 small eggs

300ml/1¼ cups milk

8 pork sausages

GET STUCK IN

1 Preheat the oven to 220°C/425°F/gas 7.

2 Place the flour and salt in a bowl. Make a well in the centre and break in the eggs.

3 Mix in half the milk using a wooden spoon. Work the mixture until smooth, then add the remainder of the milk. Beat or whisk until fully combined and the surface is covered with tiny bubbles. Set aside and allow to rest for 15–30 minutes. Whisk again before use.

4 Next, fry the sausages in a pan to lightly colour. Remove the excess fat and reserve.

5 Place the fat in a small roasting tin, adding a little oil, if needed, to bring the amount of fat up to about 4 tablespoons. Heat the fat until smoking hot, then pour in the batter.

6 Add the sausages and place into the hot oven.

7 Bake for 5–10 minutes at 220°C/425°F/gas 7, then reduce to 200°C/400°F/gas 6 and bake for 20–30 minutes or until the batter around the sausages has risen and is a deep golden brown.

8 Serve immediately or the pudding will deflate.

MAKES 4 PORTIONS

Each portion contains:

Energy	Fat	Saturates	Sugars	Salt
1042kJ **248kcals**	**11.0g**	**4.0g**	**4.4g**	**1.3g**
12%	**16%**	**20%**	**5%**	**22%**

Of your reference intake

BEEF BURGERS

STUFF YOU'LL NEED

250g/9oz best-quality minced beef

1 small red onion, finely chopped, caramelised and cooled

1 clove garlic, finely chopped, caramelised and cooled

1 tsp wholegrain mustard

1 tsp ketchup

1 tsp Worcestershire sauce

A few dashes of Tabasco sauce

1 egg, whisked

50g/½ cup breadcrumbs

10g/⅓ cup chopped parsley

Sea salt and freshly ground black pepper

Olive oil, to brush or drizzle

2 slices decent Cheddar cheese

2 burger buns, halved

1 sprig fresh thyme

Few lettuce leaves

Few slices ripe tomato

Dill pickles

GET STUCK IN

1 Mix the beef, cooked onion and garlic, mustard, ketchup, Worcestershire sauce and Tabasco together and add the egg, breadcrumbs and parsley and season well. Cook a little to check the flavour is correct.

2 Shape the mixture into 2 burger patties. Place them on a tray lined with baking parchment, cover and chill for about 30 minutes to allow them to firm up.

3 When you're ready to start cooking, brush the burgers with a little oil and then place them on the grill of a hot barbecue. Cook them for 7–10 minutes, turning halfway. Place the cheese on top of the patties and cover the burgers with the hood of the barbecue (or a stainless-steel bowl) for a minute, as this will encourage the cheese to melt down nicely.

4 In the meantime, drizzle the cut side of the burger buns with a little olive oil and sprinkle with thyme leaves. Lightly toast the burger buns, cut-side down.

Each portion contains:

Energy	Fat	Saturates	Sugars	Salt
3670kJ **876kcals**	**45.3g**	**21.0g**	**11.5g**	**3.5g**
44%	65%	105%	12%	57%

Of your reference intake

5 To assemble the burgers, sandwich the patties between the warm, toasted burger buns, and add a few slices each of lettuce, tomato and pickles. Serve with chips (see page 108).

Note: you can caramelise onions by putting them in a pan with olive oil, brown sugar and balsamic vinegar and then cook slowly for 15 minutes. Allow 1 tbsp olive oil, 1 tbsp soft brown sugar and 2 tsp balsamic vinegar per onion.

MAKES 2 PORTIONS

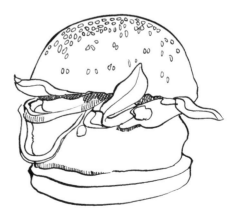

ROAST PORK BELLY WITH CARAMELISED APPLES AND MUSTARD SAUCE

STUFF YOU'LL NEED

600g/1lb 5oz pork belly, skin on and scored

1 tbsp olive oil

1 tbsp fennel seeds

1 tbsp fresh thyme leaves

2 tsp Maldon sea salt

1 small onion, sliced

60g/¼ cup butter

1 Granny Smith apple, peeled, cut in half, cored and sliced

1 glass white wine

100ml/7 tbsp cloudy apple juice

2 tsp grain mustard

50ml/3½ tbsp strong chicken stock (see page 60)

60g/¼ cup chilled butter (for the sauce)

GET STUCK IN

1 Preheat the oven to 200°C/400°F/gas 6.

2 Rub the pork belly with the olive oil, fennel seeds, thyme and salt. Place on a roasting rack. Roast in the oven for 10 minutes, then turn the oven down to 140°C/280°F/gas 2 and continue to roast for 2 hours. Once cooked, take out of the oven and leave to rest for 20–30 minutes.

3 Fry the onion in the butter for a few minutes, then make a space in the pan and add the apple slices. Caramelise on both sides. Take the apples out of the pan and reserve.

4 Return the onion to the stove, add the wine and bring to the boil. Add the apple juice and simmer, add the mustard and stock and reduce by half.

5 Whisk in the cold butter. Reserve the sauce.

6 Warm the pork and slice, serve with the caramelised apple and the sauce.

Note: this dish goes well with braised red cabbage (see page 97) and braised potatoes (see page 109).

MAKES 4 PORTIONS

Each portion contains:

Energy	Fat	Saturates	Sugars	Salt
2952kJ 712kcals	56.2g	24.6g	7.9g	3.0g
35%	80%	123%	8%	50%

Of your reference intake

BOILED BACON

1kg/2lb 4oz bacon joint (ham hock or gammon would do just fine)

1 onion, peeled

1 carrot, peeled

6 peppercorns

6 cloves

1 bay leaf

50g/¼ cup pearl barley

1 handful of fresh parsley, chopped

GET STUCK IN

1 Put the bacon in a saucepan, cover with cold water and soak for 24 hours before cooking. Change the water 3–4 times. This will draw out the salt and make the whole dish taste better. You will also be able to use the stock.

2 Place the bacon in a suitable pot and again cover with cold water. Bring to the boil and skim off the foam. Turn down to a simmer.

3 Quarter the vegetables and place in with the bacon, along with the peppercorns, cloves and bay leaf. Boil the bacon for 1½ hours.

4 When the bacon is cooked, allow it to cool in the stock.

5 Remove from the stock and remove the rind.

6 Take some stock and boil the pearl barley until tender.

7 To serve, warm the bacon in the stock, take out and slice it and place into a bowl, then ladle the stock over, place the vegetables on top and sprinkle with the barley and chopped parsley.

MAKES 4 PORTIONS

Each portion contains:

Energy 1726kJ 411kcals	Fat 19.2g	Saturates 6.3g	Sugars 3.4g	Salt 5.6g
21%	27%	32%	4%	93%

Of your reference intake

BEEF BOURGUIGNON

STUFF YOU'LL NEED

400g/14oz diced beef

25ml/2 tbsp olive oil

1 small onion, diced

2 carrots, diced

2 sticks of celery, diced

2 cloves garlic, chopped

2 sprigs fresh thyme

1 bay leaf

1 tbsp tomato purée

1 tbsp plain flour

2 large glasses red wine

500ml/2 cups beef stock

For the garnish

8 button onions

Olive oil

75g/2¾oz bacon lardons

8 button mushrooms

1 handful of fresh parsley, chopped

GET STUCK IN

1 Preheat the oven to 180°C/350°F/gas 4.

2 Make sure the meat is well trimmed of fat and sinew.

3 Heat a big pan and add the olive oil. Seal the beef by browning the meat as much as possible in the hot oil.

4 Add the onion, carrots, celery and garlic and continue to brown for 4–5 minutes.

5 Add the thyme, bay, tomato purée and flour, mix well and cook for 2–3 minutes.

6 Pour in the wine and bring to the boil. Turn down the heat and simmer for 3–4 minutes.

7 Ladle the beef, vegetables and cooking liquor into an ovenproof dish. Rinse the pot with beef stock to get the vegetables off the sides and pour on top of the beef, just enough to cover. Stir and place a lid on top of the dish and bring to the boil. Place in the oven for 4 hours or until the beef is tender.

8 In the meantime, peel the button onions and pan-fry in a little olive oil, add the bacon and brown.

Each portion contains:

Energy	Fat	Saturates	Sugars	Salt
427kJ **102kcals**	**14.8g**	**4.0g**	**5g**	**1.5g**
18%	21%	20%	5%	25%

Of your reference intake

9 Lastly, add the button mushrooms and cook for a further few minutes.

10 Take off and reserve.

11 When you are ready to serve, heat the garnish and sprinkle on top of the beef, finishing with the chopped parsley.

12 Serve with mash potatoes (see page 107) and greens.

MAKES 4 PORTIONS

PAN-FRIED STEAK

STUFF YOU'LL NEED

2 x 100–150g/ 3½–5¼oz steak of your choosing

Salt and freshly ground black pepper

1 tbsp olive oil

15g/½oz butter

GET STUCK IN

1 Heat a shallow frying pan.

2 Lightly season the steaks with salt and pepper, and drizzle with olive oil.

3 Place the steaks in the pan and seal both sides quickly, browning evenly.

4 Add the butter and baste the steak as it melts.

5 Serve with a sauce of your choosing or simply with chips (see page 108) and salad.

MAKES 2 PORTIONS

Each portion contains:

Energy 1589kJ 380kcals	Fat 21.6g	Saturates 8.3g	Sugars 0g	Salt 1.5g
19%	31%	41%	0%	25%

Of your reference intake

SAUCES & DRESSINGS

In many ways, sauces and dressings are the cornerstone of cooking. They not only moisten a dish but usually add concentrated flavours that complement the main part of the dish. Very often a sauce will cut through the richness of the meat or fish. Sauces can easily be adapted and interchanged, and it's well worth experimenting.

BASIC TOMATO SAUCE

STUFF YOU'LL NEED

4 tbsp olive oil

4 cloves garlic, finely sliced

1 bunch of fresh basil, leaves picked and torn

3 x 400g/14oz tins good-quality whole plum tomatoes

Sea salt and freshly ground black pepper

GET STUCK IN

1 Place a large non-stick frying pan on the heat and pour in 4 generous glugs of olive oil. Add the garlic and cook until it begins to colour lightly.

2 Add the basil and tomatoes. Using the back of a wooden spoon, mush and squash the tomatoes as much as you can.

3 Season the sauce with salt and pepper. As soon as it comes to the boil, remove the pan from the heat. Strain the sauce through a coarse sieve into a bowl. Use your wooden spoon to push any larger bits of tomato through. Discard the basil and garlic that will be left in the sieve, but make sure you scrape any of the tomato sauce off the back of the sieve into the bowl.

4 Pour the sauce back into the pan and bring to the boil. Turn down the heat and simmer for 5 minutes to concentrate the flavours. It will be ready when it's the perfect consistency for spreading on your pizza (see page 100).

5 Store the sauce in a clean jar in the fridge – it'll keep for a week or so. Also, it's great to freeze in batches or even in an ice cube tray, so you can defrost exactly the amount you need. But to be honest, it's so quick to make, you might as well make it on the day you need it.

MAKES 500ML

Each portion contains:

Energy	Fat	Saturates	Sugars	Salt
848kJ **202kcals**	**11.7g**	**1.6g**	**16.1g**	**0.6g**
10%	**17%**	**8%**	**18%**	**10%**

Of your reference intake

RICH TOMATO SAUCE

STUFF YOU'LL NEED

- 15 ripe plum tomatoes
- 1 tbsp olive oil
- 1 large white onion, finely chopped
- 3 cloves garlic, finely chopped
- 1 glass white wine
- 1 tsp tomato purée
- 1 sprig fresh rosemary, needles chopped
- Salt and freshly ground black pepper

GET STUCK IN

1 Firstly deseed the tomatoes by cutting them in half and squeezing. This will get out most of the seeds but you don't have to get them all. Discard the seeds. Cut the tomato halves into a rough dice and put the chopped tomatoes to one side.

2 Heat the olive oil in a heavy-based pan over a medium heat. Add the chopped onion and garlic and cook without colouring until they turn translucent, turning down the heat if necessary.

3 Pour in the white wine and bring to the boil. Add the tomato purée and the rosemary and cook for a further minute before adding the tomatoes.

4 Cook on a low heat for approximately 30 minutes until the sauce has combined and become a little thicker.

5 Check the seasoning by taste and serve with your favourite pasta (see pages 76–7) and a chunk of fresh, warm, crusty bread.

Note: you can purée the sauce if a smoother style is preferred. Add different herbs and spices to vary the flavour.

MAKES 4 PORTIONS

Each portion contains:

Energy	Fat	Saturates	Sugars	Salt
529kJ **126kcals**	**3.2g**	**0.5g**	**13.0g**	**<0.1g**
6%	**5%**	**2%**	**14%**	**0%**

Of your reference intake

PESTO

STUFF YOU'LL NEED

40g/1½oz fresh basil leaves

125ml/½ cup extra virgin olive oil

5 cloves garlic, peeled

50g/⅓ cup pine nuts, toasted

50g/⅔ cup Parmesan cheese, grated

Salt and freshly ground black pepper

GET STUCK IN

1 Pick the basil off the stalks and whizz in a blender with the extra virgin olive oil.

2 Add the garlic and pine nuts and finally the Parmesan, and whizz until relatively smooth. Taste and season with salt and pepper.

Note: throw this sauce into lots of hot steaming pasta (see pages 76–7), or drizzle over freshly sliced tomatoes and mozzarella cheese to make an amazing salad.

MAKES 4 PORTIONS

Each portion contains:

Energy	Fat	Saturates	Sugars	Salt
1762kJ 427kcals	43.6g	7.5g	0.6g	0.7g
21%	62%	38%	1%	1%

Of your reference intake

VINAIGRETTE

STUFF YOU'LL NEED

1 tbsp lemon juice

1 tbsp white wine vinegar

1 tsp Dijon mustard

1 tsp honey

Freshly ground black pepper

3 tbsp extra virgin olive oil or light rapeseed oil

GET STUCK IN

1 Find a clean jar with a lid that screws on firmly.

2 Mix the lemon juice, vinegar, mustard, honey and seasoning in the jar until smoothly combined.

3 Pour in the oil, put the lid on and shake the jar until blended.

Note: this is a good all-rounder for any type of salad and you can keep it in the fridge for ages.

MAKES 8 PORTIONS

Each portion contains:

Energy	Fat	Saturates	Sugars	Salt
319kJ	**8.3g**	**0.9g**	**0.5g**	**0.07g**
77kcals				
4%	12%	4%	1%	1%

Of your reference intake

GRAVY

STUFF YOU'LL NEED

- 500ml/2 cups good brown meat stock
- 1 bay leaf
- 30ml/2 tbsp olive oil
- 200g/7oz meat trimmings if any, chopped up
- 25g/⅛ cup butter
- 1 large carrot, finely diced
- 1 shallot, finely diced
- 1 stick of celery, finely diced
- 1 clove garlic, finely chopped
- ⅓ leek, finely diced
- 1 tsp tomato purée
- 100ml/7 tbsp white or red wine
- 3 sprigs fresh thyme
- Salt and freshly ground black pepper

GET STUCK IN

1 Put the meat stock on to boil with a bay leaf in it.

2 In a heavy pan, heat the oil. Add any meat trimmings you may have and sauté until cooked and the meat is browned.

3 Remove the meat from the pan, draining most of the fat.

4 Add the butter to the pan, followed by all the vegetables. Sauté until lightly coloured all over, put the meat back into the pan (if using), add the tomato purée and cook for a further 3 minutes. Then add the white or red wine and reduce to the consistency of syrup.

5 Add the hot stock and thyme, bring to the boil, then turn down the heat and simmer until reduced by half, skimming off any impurities that rise to the surface.

6 Drain through a fine sieve. Season the gravy and serve.

MAKES 4 PORTIONS

Each portion contains:

Energy	Fat	Saturates	Sugars	Salt
1041kJ 251kcals	18.5g	7.2g	1.6g	0.8g
13%	26%	36%	2%	14%

Of your reference intake

WHITE SAUCE

STUFF YOU'LL NEED

425ml/1¾ cups milk

A few parsley stalks

1 bay leaf

10 black peppercorns

1 onion studded with a clove

40g/3 tbsp butter

30g/¼ cup plain flour

Salt and freshly ground black pepper

GET STUCK IN

1 Place the milk in a saucepan and add the parsley stalks, the bay leaf, peppercorns and onion. Bring to the boil, turn down the heat and simmer for 5 minutes, then strain.

2 In the same pan, melt the butter and add the flour. Cook until a sandy texture is achieved. Keep cooking until the paste comes away from the pan cleanly.

3 Slowly add the infused milk, mixing well. Repeat until it's all in and the sauce has a nice thick consistency.

4 Simmer the sauce gently for 25 minutes, stirring frequently to stop it sticking to the bottom of the pan. Season with salt and pepper.

5 When the sauce is finished, strain and cover with cling film to stop it skinning over. Cool before refrigerating.

Note: you can use this sauce in many dishes, such as lasagne and vegetable side dishes. You can also try adding mushrooms, herbs and grated cheese.

MAKES 4 PORTIONS

Each portion contains:

Energy	Fat	Saturates	Sugars	Salt
590kJ 142kcals	10.0g	6.4g	5.0g	1.5g
7%	14%	32%	6%	26%

Of your reference intake

BREAD

Bread plays a huge cultural part in our lives. I love cooking bread for my family and friends, and I think it makes a lovely gift as it's something that can be made easily with your hands. There are a few simple things to remember when making bread.

Basically all you need is flour, yeast, water, sugar and salt. A nice warm atmosphere will help the yeast to prove (grow), so using warm ingredients helps with that process.

Salt helps make the dough more manageable and easier to eat. Some cultures traditionally don't use salt and, as a result, their bread is quite tough.

You can use most flours for bread, but strong flour contains a large amount of energy, vitamins and minerals, while wholemeal has fibre and so is generally regarded as healthier.

Once you have combined your ingredients together, this is called dough. It's important to knead the dough in order to stretch the gluten (protein); this also helps gain a nice crumb and good texture.

BASIC WHITE BREAD

STUFF YOU'LL NEED

15g/½oz yeast (you can usually get this fresh from a good supermarket, or you can use the dried equivalent)

300ml/1¼ cups warm water

5g/1 tsp sugar

30ml/2 tbsp olive oil

500g/3½ cups strong white flour

10g/2 tsp salt

1 egg, whisked, for wash

Poppy, sunflower or sesame seeds

GET STUCK IN

1 Dissolve the yeast in the water and add the sugar and the olive oil. Mix well.

2 Place the flour and salt in a large bowl and make a well. Using a spoon, start to pour the yeast mixture into the flour, stirring all the time. Stir until it forms a ball.

3 Sprinkle the dough with a little flour and bring it together with your hands. Place the dough on a floured surface and start to knead, pulling and pushing the dough to stretch it back and forth. This will take about 10 minutes. When the dough has a nice smooth texture, it has been kneaded enough.

4 Place in a bowl and cover with a warm, damp tea towel and leave in a warm place for 25 minutes or until it has doubled in size.

5 Place the dough back on the floured surface and knock it back by kneading it once again, this time for 2–3 minutes.

6 Cut the bread into 12 even-sized pieces and cover with a damp tea towel. This creates a warm, damp atmosphere to aid the proving. This should take about 20 minutes.

7 Shape the pieces of dough and place them on a lined baking sheet.

8 Prove under the damp tea towel again until the dough has doubled in size and brush with the egg wash. Scatter with the seeds.

9 Bake at 220°C/425°F/gas 7 for 8–10 minutes. The loaf should sound hollow when tapped underneath and be golden brown.

Note: once you have mastered this basic bread dough, you can experiment using various flavours, flours and oils to develop your own style of bread.

MAKES 12 ROLLS

BAKING TIPS

Allowing the dough to prove in a warm and moist atmosphere will help the yeast to rise and become light and airy when it's baking.

I usually egg wash the dough before cooking. This provides a nice golden colour, but milk will do just fine and a dusting of flour gives a rustic look.

Each portion contains:

Energy	Fat	Saturates	Sugars	Salt
1063kJ **253kcals**	**4.5g**	**0.6g**	**1.5g**	**1.3g**
13%	**6%**	**3%**	**2%**	**22%**

Of your reference intake

HONEY AND HEMPSEED BREAD

STUFF YOU'LL NEED

325g/2⅓ cups strong flour
(wholemeal or white)

5g/1 tsp sea salt

7g/¼oz easy bake yeast

15ml/1 tbsp hempseed oil
(optional)

200ml/¾ cup very warm
water (3 parts boiling –
1 part cold)

10ml/2 tsp honey

45g/3 tbsp hemp seeds,
half crushed in a pestle
and mortar, half kept
whole

1 egg, whisked, for wash

GET STUCK IN

1 Preheat the oven to 220°C/425°F/gas 7.

2 In a warm bowl mix the flour, salt and yeast. Add the oil, water, honey and half the crushed hemp seeds, and mix to a soft dough. Knead for 10 minutes on a floured surface.

3 Place in a floured bowl and place a damp towel over. Prove for at least 15 minutes or until doubled in size. Lightly knead once again on a floured surface.

4 If making loaves, shape evenly and place into a warmed 450g/1lb dough tin. For rolls divide evenly into 50g/2oz balls and place on baking sheets.

5 Cover and leave to rise in a warm place for 15 minutes or until doubled in size.

6 Egg wash the surface of the loaves or rolls and sprinkle with the remaining hemp seeds.

7 Place in the middle of the oven for 30 minutes (15 minutes for rolls). Remove from the oven and place onto a wire rack.

MAKES 1 LOAF/ 8 SMALL ROLLS

Each portion contains:

Energy	Fat	Saturates	Sugars	Salt
883kJ 210kcals	5.7g	0.9g	2.1g	0.7g
11%	8%	4%	2%	11%

Of your reference intake

SHARING FOOD

Food is all about togetherness. Why not have shared or themed nights in with your mates? For example, make a few pizzas, a couple of great fresh salads and a pud to finish. You can all get stuck into making the dough and toppings. Then you can enjoy the results while chatting over a few beers or a bottle of wine, watching a film or playing a game. It's far better than blowing your money on a crazy night out that you'll only have forgotten in the morning!

Whether you're living with friends or family, or just inviting your mates round, there's nothing better than to stick a massive bowl of deliciousness that you've made together in the middle of the table and digging in.

So...

Light a few candles

Share the cost

Save money rather than eating out

Do the washing up together

Have a lot of fun theming the evening

You could even play your own version of *Come Dine With Me*...!

PIZZA

Pizza must be the ultimate sharing dish. There nothing like freshly made pizza, served straight from the oven.

Try this Place the cheese straight on the dough and bake until nicely browned, then place the garnish on top and continue cooking. Serve the sauce as a dip and you will be well impressed with the difference, believe me. The dough stays really crisp and the cheese has that really great savoury, toasted flavour.

PIZZA DOUGH

Makes 6–8 pizzas | Prep time: 20 minutes | Cook time: 10 minutes each

STUFF YOU'LL NEED

350g/2½ cups strong white flour

100g/¾ cup wholemeal flour

30g/⅓ cup oatmeal

1 level tbsp fine sea salt

2 tsp extra virgin olive oil

15g/½oz dried yeast

2 tsp sugar

325ml/1¹/₃ cups warm water

GET STUCK IN

1 Sift the white and wholemeal flours into a large bowl. Mix the oatmeal, salt, oil, yeast, sugar and warm water in a jug and leave for 2 minutes.

2 When the yeast mixture is fully combined, add it to the flour bit by bit until dough is formed; this then needs to be kneaded until the dough is smooth and silky.

3 Place the dough in a well-floured bowl and cover with a damp cloth. Put in a warm place to prove. When the dough has doubled in size it is ready.

4 It's a good idea to roll the pizzas out 15–20 minutes before you want to cook them; don't roll them out and leave them hanging around for a few hours. However, if you are working in advance it's better to cover your dough in cling film and leave in the fridge. If you want

to get them rolled out so there's one less thing to do when your friends have arrived, simply roll the dough into rough circles, about ½cm/⅕ in thick, and place them on slightly larger pieces of tin foil which have been rubbed with olive oil and dusted with flour. You can then stack the pizzas, cover them with cling film and pop them into the fridge.

5 When you are ready to cook, place each pizza on a tray, spoon tomato sauce (see pages 149–50) on and around the base to make sure it goes to the edge, then chuck on your favourite toppings. Put them in a hot oven (200°C/400°F/gas 6) until crisp on the underside and toasted at the edges.

TOPPINGS

Here are some of my favourite pizza varieties to start you off.

- Mozzarella and cherry tomatoes with fresh basil
- Green and red grapes, rosemary, pine nuts and ricotta
- Egg, ham, tinned artichokes, olives, mozzarella, tomato sauce and basil
- Roasted potatoes, peppers, mozzarella, thyme and tomatoes
- Shredded roast chicken with thyme, taleggio and lemon-dressed rocket
- Smoked bacon, mozzarella, fresh chilli and tomatoes
- Spicy salami, courgette, basil, tomato and mozzarella

Each portion contains:

Energy	Fat	Saturates	Sugars	Salt
1320kJ 310kcals	2.7g	0.5g	2.0g	1.6g
16%	4%	2%	2%	27%

Of your reference intake

THAI CURRY & SATAY + CHICKEN SATAY

Serves 4 | Prep time: 1 hour | Cook time: 30 minutes

THAI CURRY & SATAY

STUFF YOU'LL NEED

200ml/¾ cup coconut milk

3 tbsp Thai green paste

2 tbsp honey

Juice of 1 lime

450g/1lb mini chicken fillets

1 handful of green beans

1 handful of fresh coriander

1 red chilli, deseeded and finely chopped

Cooked basmati rice (see page 80)

GET STUCK IN

1 Pour the coconut milk into a shallow, non-metallic dish. Add the Thai paste, honey and lime juice and mix well. Add the chicken, toss well and set aside for 15 minutes.

2 Transfer to a saucepan and gently simmer for 12–15 minutes until the chicken is cooked through and the sauce has thickened slightly. Add the green beans.

3 Garnish with coriander and the chilli, if you like, and serve with cooked basmati rice.

CHICKEN SATAY

2 tbsp chunky peanut butter (without palm oil or sugar)

1 clove garlic, finely grated

1 tsp Madras curry powder

A few shakes soy sauce

2 tsp lime juice

2 skinless, boneless chicken breast fillets (about 300g/10½oz) cut into thick strips about 10cm/4in long

Cucumber, cut into fingers

Sweet chilli sauce, to serve

GET STUCK IN

1 Preheat oven to 200°C/400°F/gas 6 and line a baking tray with non-stick paper.

2 Mix the peanut butter with the garlic, curry powder, soy sauce and lime juice in a bowl. Some nut butters are thicker than others so, if necessary, add a dash of boiling water to get a coating consistency. Add the chicken strips, mix well then arrange on the baking sheet, spaced apart, and bake in the oven for 8–10 minutes until cooked, but still juicy.

3 Eat warm with the cucumber sticks and chilli sauce, or leave to cool then keep in the fridge for up to 2 days.

Each portion contains:

Energy	Fat	Saturates	Sugar	Salt
626kJ **310kcals**	**5.3g**	**1.2g**	**4.5g**	**0.26g**
16%	**4%**	**2%**	**5%**	**4%**

Of your reference intake

INDIAN-SPICED GLAZED CHICKEN WINGS + CHICKPEA CURRY

MEAL THREE

Serves 4 | Prep time: 45 minutes | Cook time: 1 hour

INDIAN-SPICED GLAZED CHICKEN WINGS

STUFF YOU'LL NEED

500g/1lb 2oz chicken wings

100g/¾ cup plain flour

vegetable oil, for deep-frying

For the marinade

1 tsp paprika

½ tsp ground cumin

¼ tsp ground coriander

¼ tsp garam masala

½ egg, whisked

¼ tsp Dijon mustard

½ tsp vegetable oil, plus extra for shallow-frying

GET STUCK IN

1 Mix all the ingredients for the marinade together in a large bowl and add the chicken wings. Cover and place in the fridge for at least 1 hour.

2 For the Indian-spiced glaze sauce. Put the tamarind in a bowl, pour over the warm water and leave to soak for 10 minutes until softened.

3 Heat the vegetable oil in a large saucepan over a medium heat, then add the onion and cook, stirring occasionally, until soft, for about 5 minutes. Stir in the powdered and crushed spices and cook for 5 minutes, stirring often, then stir in the tomato purée and cook for a further 3 minutes.

4 Add the sugar, honey, tomato ketchup, Worcestershire sauce, vinegar, chicken stock pot and water to the pan and stir to combine. Drain the softened tamarind, discarding the liquid, and add it to the pan. Bring to the boil over a medium heat, then turn down the heat and cook for 10 minutes.

For the Indian-spiced glaze

40g/1½oz dried tamarind

250ml/1 cup warm water

1 tbsp vegetable oil

1 medium white onion, sliced

½ tsp dried chilli flakes

1 tsp fennel seeds

1 tsp cumin seeds

1 tsp coriander seeds

1 tbsp tomato purée

30g/$^1/_8$ cup light soft brown sugar

45g/$^1/_8$ cup runny honey

2 tbsp tomato ketchup

75ml/$^1/_3$ cup Worcestershire sauce

20ml/1½ tbsp white wine vinegar

1 chicken stock pot/cube plus 250ml/1 cup water

To garnish

2 spring onions, chopped

1 handful of fresh coriander leaves, chopped

5 Once the chicken wings have had time to marinate, remove them from the fridge and dust each wing in flour to coat, making sure you tap off any excess.

6 Fill a large saucepan one-third full of vegetable oil and heat until a cube of bread dropped in the oil sizzles and turns golden in 30 seconds.

7 Deep-fry the wings (in several batches) in the hot oil for about 4–6 minutes until cooked through and golden all over. Remove with a slotted spoon and drain on kitchen paper. Keep warm in a low oven while you cook the rest in the same way, making sure you bring the oil back up to temperature for each batch.

8 Once all the chicken wings are cooked, coat the wings in the warm, sticky Indian sauce, then pile them onto a serving platter. Garnish with the spring onions and chopped coriander before serving.

Each portion contains:

Energy	Fat	Saturates	Sugar	Salt
972kJ **232kcals**	**12g**	**2.5g**	**9.7g**	**0.77g**
12%	19%	13%	11%	13%

Of your reference intake

CHICKPEA CURRY

STUFF YOU'LL NEED

2 tbsp oil

1 onion, diced

1 tsp fresh or dried chilli,
to taste

9 garlic cloves (approx.
1 small bulb of garlic),
peeled

Thumb-sized piece of fresh
root ginger, peeled

1 tbsp ground coriander

2 tbsp ground cumin

1 tbsp garam masala

2 tbsp tomato purée

½ tsp salt

For the curry

2 x 400g/14oz tins
chickpeas, drained

400g/14oz tin chopped
tomatoes

100g/3½oz creamed
coconut

1 handful of fresh
coriander, chopped, plus
extra to garnish

100g/3½oz spinach

Pilau rice, to serve
(see page 80)

GET STUCK IN

1 To make the paste, heat a little of the oil in a frying pan, add the onion and chilli and cook until softened, for about 8 minutes. Meanwhile, in a food processor, roughly combine the garlic, ginger and remaining oil, then add the spices, tomato purée, salt and the fried onion. Blend to a smooth paste – add a drop of water or more oil, if needed.

2 Cook the paste in a medium saucepan for 2 minutes over a medium-high heat, stirring occasionally so it doesn't stick. Tip in the chickpeas and chopped tomatoes and simmer for 5 minutes until reduced down. Add the coconut with a little water, cook for 5 minutes more, then add the coriander and spinach, and cook until wilted. Garnish with extra coriander and serve with pilau rice.

GRILLED CORN WITH CHILLI & FETA + STICKY RIBS

Serves 4 | Prep time: 30 minutes | Cook time: 2 hours

GRILLED CORN WITH CHILLI & FETA

STUFF YOU'LL NEED

Olive oil, for frying

4 whole corn on the cobs, husks removed

3-4 tbsp water

80g/⅓ cup butter, softened

1-2 dried chipotle chillies, rehydrated and finely chopped

2 tbsp chopped coriander leaves

Sea salt and freshly ground black pepper

4 tbsp crumbled feta cheese

Lime wedges, to serve

GET STUCK IN

1 Heat a large, heavy frying pan over a medium heat. Add a little oil and gently cook the cobs in the pan for about 5 minutes until coloured and lightly charred all over. Add the water to the pan and continue to cook over a medium heat for about 8 minutes until the liquid has evaporated and the corn is cooked through (turn down the heat if it starts to colour too much).

2 Meanwhile, mix together the butter, chillies, coriander and a little seasoning.

3 Once the corn is cooked, remove and cover with knobs of the seasoned butter, allowing it to melt over the corn. Sprinkle over the feta cheese and serve with wedges of lime.

Each portion contains:

Energy	Fat	Saturates	Sugar	Salt
692kJ 166kcals	9.3g	3.9g	12g	1.4g
8%	13%	19%	14%	23%

Of your reference intake

STICKY RIBS

STUFF YOU'LL NEED

1 onion

2 cloves garlic

2 tbsp olive oil

½ tsp chilli flakes (optional)

1 tsp fennel seeds

110g/½ cup dark soft brown sugar

600g/2⅔ cups tomato ketchup

110ml/½ cup dark soy sauce

1kg/2lb 4oz rack of pork spare ribs

GET STUCK IN

1 Preheat the oven to 150°C/300°F/gas 2.

2 While the oven is warming, roughly chop the onion. Then crush the garlic in a garlic crusher.

3 Place a frying pan over a medium heat until it is hot, then add the olive oil, onion and garlic. Fry for 4–5 minutes or until the onion has softened.

4 Add the chilli (if using), fennel seeds and brown sugar and cook, stirring for a further 1–2 minutes until the sugar has dissolved.

5 Add the tomato ketchup and soy sauce and stir everything together. Bring to the boil, then turn down the heat and simmer for 10 minutes until the sauce thickens.

6 Put the ribs into a deep-sided roasting tray and pour over the sauce.

7 Cover the tray with foil and put it into the oven for 2 hours, then increase the oven temperature to 180°C/350°F/gas 4, remove the foil and cook for 30–45 minutes more.

8 Once cooked, remove the tray from the oven and let the ribs cool down so they are not too hot to handle before serving.

9 Serve with lots of paper napkins because sticky fingers are guaranteed!

BEEF TACOS + MEXICAN COLESLAW

Serves 4 | Prep time: 1 hour | Cook time: 30 mins

BEEF TACOS

STUFF YOU'LL NEED

1 onion

1 red pepper

1 green pepper

1 tbsp olive oil

2 cloves garlic

Pinch of paprika

1½ tsp cumin seeds

500g/1lb 2oz quality minced beef (5% fat)

250ml/1 cup beef stock made from a stock pot cube

12 corn taco shells

For the salsa

2 ripe tomatoes

1 spring onion

3 sprigs fresh coriander

Juice of ½ lime

Salt and freshly ground black pepper

Guacamole

2 ripe avocados

Juice of ½ lime

2 tbsp crème fraîche

GET STUCK IN

1 Dice the onion, then deseed and dice the peppers. Soften in the olive oil in a large pan over a low heat.

2 Finely slice the garlic and add to the pan along with the paprika and cumin. Cook for 1–2 minutes, then add the beef and stir until it has browned.

3 Pour in the stock, cover and cook for 45 minutes or until reduced and delicious.

4 Preheat the oven to 180°C/350°F/gas 4.

5 For the salsa, roughly chop the tomatoes, finely slice the spring onion, then pick and roughly chop the coriander leaves. Combine with the lime juice, then season carefully to taste.

6 For the guacamole, halve and stone the avocados, then mash the flesh with a fork. Squeeze in the lime juice, add the crème fraîche, season and gently mix it all up.

7 Spread the taco shells out on a baking tray and place in the oven for 3–4 minutes until crisp.

8 Fill the shells with the meat, salsa and guacamole or lay everything out and let everyone help themselves.

MEXICAN COLESLAW

STUFF YOU'LL NEED

¼ small white cabbage

¼ small red cabbage

1 small bunch of radishes (about 5), finely sliced

1 carrot, finely sliced

½ large bunch of fresh coriander, leaves and stalks finely chopped

1 large jalapeño chilli (or other green chilli), to taste, finely sliced

½ red onion, finely sliced

1 x 200g/7oz tin sweetcorn

1 x 400g/14oz tin black-eyed beans, rinsed

2-3 tbsp extra virgin olive oil

Juice of 2-3 limes

Sea salt

GET STUCK IN

1 Shred the white and red cabbages into two separate piles. Put just the white cabbage into a large bowl with the radishes, carrot and most of the coriander. Mix everything together really well, then kick up the flavours by adding almost all the chopped chilli, the sliced red onion, sweetcorn and the washed black-eyed beans and a few tablespoons of extra virgin olive oil.

2 Add most of the lime juice and a good pinch of salt, then toss together and have a taste. Just keep adjusting everything, adding more fragrance with the coriander, heat with the last of the chilli and a dash of lime juice, until it's just right for you.

3 When you're happy, fold in the red cabbage right before serving so it doesn't stain everything, and tuck in.

Each portion contains:

Energy 669kJ 160kcals	Fat 8.9g	Saturates 3.5g	Sugar 2.0g	Salt 0.75g
8%	13%	18%	2%	12%

Of your reference intake

PRAWN STIR-FRY + TEMPURA VEGETABLES WITH SHERRY SOY DIPPING SAUCE

Serves 4 | Prep time: 30 minutes | Cook time: 1 hour

PRAWN STIR-FRY

STUFF YOU'LL NEED

- 250g/9oz egg noodles
- 2 tbsp rapeseed oil
- 1 red pepper, deseeded and sliced
- 1 bunch of spring onions, cut into 2cm/⁴/₅in pieces
- 100g/3½oz mangetout
- 1 tbsp tomato purée
- 2 tbsp light soy sauce
- 2 tbsp Thai sweet chilli sauce
- 1 tbsp clear honey
- 250g/9oz tiger prawns, cooked and peeled

GET STUCK IN

1 Cook the noodles in boiling water for 4–5 minutes until tender, then drain.

2 Meanwhile, heat the oil in a large frying pan and fry the vegetables for 4–5 minutes.

3 Blend the tomato purée with the soy, chilli sauce and honey and stir into the vegetables with the prawns. Cook for 1–2 minutes, then gently stir in the noodles and serve.

Each portion contains:

Energy	Fat	Saturates	Sugar	Salt
717kJ 170kcals	5.1g	0.4g	5.9	1.6
8%	7%	2%	7%	26%

Of your reference intake

TEMPURA VEGETABLES WITH SHERRY SOY DIPPING SAUCE

STUFF YOU'LL NEED

100g/3½oz (approx.) each of a mix of firm vegetables, such as aubergine, broccoli, courgette, mushrooms, red pepper and sweet potatoes, cut into bite-size pieces

Groundnut or sunflower oil, for deep-frying

For the tempura batter

85g/⅔ cup plain flour

1 tbsp cornflour

½ tsp fine sea salt

300ml/1¼ cups mineral water

For the dipping sauce

3 tbsp soy sauce

3 tbsp dry sherry

1 tbsp sugar

1 lemon, zest only

GET STUCK IN

1 Preheat the oven to 150°C/300°F/gas 2. Mix together the sauce ingredients in a small bowl. Make the batter (see step 4, below). Cover a baking tray with sheets of kitchen paper. Start to heat a deep-fat frying pan or large wok a third full of oil and have the frying basket, or slotted spoon, to hand.

2 When the oil reaches 190°C/375°F dip some of the prepared veg briefly into the batter, shake off any excess, then lower straight into the hot oil. Don't crowd the frying basket. Fry for about 2 minutes until light golden and crisp, then drain on kitchen paper.

3 Repeat with the remaining vegetables in batches, dipping into the batter just before you fry them and remember to let the oil heat back up to the correct temperature between each batch. Keep the tempura warm in the oven, leaving the door slightly ajar so that they stay crisp. They are best served immediately on a warm plate with the sauce alongside for dipping.

4 Make the tempura batter just as you are about to cook. Sift the plain flour and cornflour with the sea salt into a large mixing bowl. Whisk in the ice-cold sparkling mineral water along with a few ice cubes, but don't over beat.

LEMON DRIZZLE POPCORN + CHOCOLATE BROWNIE

Serves 4 | Prep time: 1 hour | Cook time: 30 minutes

LEMON DRIZZLE POPCORN

STUFF YOU'LL NEED

500g/2½ cups caster sugar

100g/3½oz citrus powder

2 vanilla pods

Zest from 2 large lemons

A few splashes of olive oil

2 knobs of butter

200g/3⅓ cups popcorn kernels

GET STUCK IN

1 Empty the caster sugar into a mixing bowl. Stir in the citrus powder, the seeds from the vanilla pods and lemon zest.

2 Add the vanilla pods to the bowl and bash them up a bit with a wooden spoon to release extra flavour.

3 Transfer the mixture to an airtight container and pop the lid on. This mix will keep for a long time.

4 Get a large pan with a lid, add a few glugs of olive oil and the butter. Place on a high heat. Once the butter has melted, stir in the popcorn kernels. Put the lid straight on and leave for a couple of minutes to get going.

5 When it starts popping, give the pan a shake every 30 seconds or so, holding the lid firmly in place, making sure all of the kernels pop.

6 When the popping stops, turn the heat off. Add 6 tablespoons of the flavoured sugar, pop the lid back on and shake well to coat.

7 Tip the spiced popcorn into a large bowl or lots of small bowls and tuck in.

CHOCOLATE BROWNIE

STUFF YOU'LL NEED

250g/1 cup unsalted butter

200g/7oz dark Fairtrade chocolate (70% cocoa solids), broken up

75g/½ cup dried sour cherries (optional)

50g/⅓ cup chopped nuts (optional)

80g/⅔ cup cocoa powder, sifted

65g/½ cup plain flour, sifted

1 tsp baking powder

360g/1¾ cups caster sugar

4 large free-range or organic eggs

Zest of 1 orange (optional)

250ml/1 cup crème fraîche (optional)

GET STUCK IN

1 Preheat the oven to 180°C/350°F/gas 4.

2 Line a 25cm/10in square baking tin with greaseproof paper.

3 In a large bowl over some simmering water, melt the butter and the chocolate and mix until smooth.

4 Add the cherries and nuts, if you're using them, and stir together.

5 In a separate bowl, mix together the cocoa powder, flour, baking powder and sugar, then add this to the chocolate, cherry and nut mixture. Stir together well.

6 Beat the eggs and mix in until you have a silky consistency.

7 Pour your brownie mix into the baking tray, and place in the oven for around 25 minutes. You don't want to overcook them so, unlike cakes, you don't want a skewer to come out all clean. The brownies should be slightly springy on the outside but still gooey in the middle.

8 Allow to cool in the tray, then carefully transfer to a large chopping board and cut into chunky squares.

Each portion contains:

Energy	Fat	Saturates	Sugar	Salt
1848kJ 440kcals	19g	11g	49g	0.36g
22%	27%	52%	53%	6%

Of your reference intake

174

MY PERSONAL FAVOURITES

H ere are a few additional recipes from my own home. They're designed to please your taste buds while also doing some good to your mind and body. They're fairly simple and once you've done some of the basic recipes in the book, these should be right up your street.

BREAKFAST

I have banged on about breakfast already, but here are some simple ideas that won't only get you going, but keep you going until lunchtime. Don't forget to make it a pleasure and not a chore, so get organised and pre-prepare stuff like the granola.

BANANA AND RASPBERRY SMOOTHIE WITH GREEK YOGHURT AND HONEY

Serves 4 | Prep time: 10 minutes

STUFF YOU'LL NEED

568ml/2½ cups organic milk

300ml/1¼ cups organic Greek-style yoghurt

2 organic bananas

300g/2½ cups organic raspberries

2 tbsp organic honey

GET STUCK IN

1 Place all the ingredients in a blender and blend until smooth. Serve straight away, garnished with a few extra raspberries.

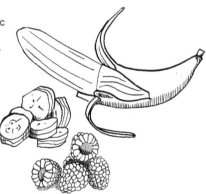

Each portion contains:

Energy	Fat	Saturates	Sugars	Salt
1063kJ 253kcals	10.4g	6.7g	28.4g	0.3g
13%	15%	34%	32%	5%

Of your reference intake

APPLE, LEMON AND HONEY MUESLI WITH RASPBERRIES AND ALMONDS

Serves 4 | Prep time: 5 minutes | Soak time: overnight

STUFF YOU'LL NEED

- 125g/1½ cups porridge oats
- 100g/3½oz granola (see page 18)
- 300ml/1¼ cups cold milk
- 100ml/7 tbsp apple juice
- 225ml/1 cup natural yoghurt
- 3 tbsp clear honey
- Zest of 1 lemon
- 2 dessert apples, peeled and grated
- 1 generous handful of fresh or frozen raspberries, defrosted overnight
- 1 handful of toasted almonds

GET STUCK IN

1 Mix the oats, granola, milk and fruit juice together in a bowl. Cover and leave in the fridge overnight.

2 In the morning, stir in the yoghurt, honey, lemon zest and grated apples, then top with the raspberries and almonds.

Note: you can add any of your favourite fruit.

Each portion contains:

Energy	Fat	Saturates	Sugars	Salt
1617kJ **385kcals**	**9.5g**	**1.8g**	**28.7g**	**0.2g**
19%	14%	9%	32%	3%

Of your reference intake

POACHED EGGS ON TOAST WITH GRILLED BACON

Serves 2 | Prep time: 5 minutes | Cook time: 5 minutes

STUFF YOU'LL NEED

4 rashers lean back bacon

4 slices wholemeal bread with seeds

Butter or low-fat spread for the toast

1 tsp vinegar

Pinch of salt

4 medium free-range eggs

GET STUCK IN

1 Heat the grill, place the bacon on a non-stick baking tray and place under the grill. Cook on both sides until crisp and golden and then drain on kitchen paper to remove excess fat. Keep warm.

2 Meanwhile fill the kettle and put on to boil. Toast the bread and spread with your choice of spread. Keep warm.

3 Fill a frying pan with boiling water from the kettle and put on the stove. Add the vinegar and salt and heat until it is very gently simmering. Crack the eggs and carefully drop them into the water. Cook gently for 3–4 minutes depending how you like your eggs.

4 Remove the pan from the heat. Use a slotted spoon to lift the eggs from the water, drain and arrange on two plates with the toast.

5 Serve with a glass of orange juice.

Each portion contains:

Energy	Fat	Saturates	Sugars	Salt
2156kJ 517kcals	31.2g	12.6g	1.7g	3.8g
26%	45%	63%	2%	64%

Of your reference intake

SIMPLE BAGELS WITH SCRAMBLED EGG AND PLUM TOMATOES

Serves 1 | Prep time: 5 minutes | Cook time: 5 minutes

STUFF YOU'LL NEED

- 1 wholemeal bagel
- 2 large eggs
- Dash of milk
- A knob of butter
- Freshly ground black pepper
- 1 vine-ripened plum tomato, sliced

GET STUCK IN

1 Cut the bagel in half and lightly toast the bready side.

2 Meanwhile, crack open the eggs and whisk with a dash of milk and the butter. Cook on a medium heat whisking to make a scrambled egg. Season with pepper.

3 Slice the tomato, place a layer on the bagel and top with the scrambled egg.

4 Place the top on the bagel and serve.

Each portion contains:

Energy	Fat	Saturates	Sugars	Salt
2096kJ 499kcals	19.7g	6.6g	7.0g	3.5g
25%	28%	33%	8%	58%

Of your reference intake

VERY FRUITY COMPOTE WITH YOGHURT

Serves 4 | Prep time: 10 minutes | Cook time: 30 minutes

STUFF YOU'LL NEED

225g/2 cups fresh rhubarb, chopped

300ml/1¼ cups water

50g/¼ cup soft unrefined light brown sugar

400g/2⅔ cups dried fruit mix (e.g. apricots, apples, pears, prunes)

120ml/½ cup low-fat natural yoghurt, to serve

GET STUCK IN

1 Preheat the oven to 180°C/350°F/gas 4.

2 Place the rhubarb in a saucepan with the sugar and water. Simmer for 5 minutes or until the rhubarb starts to soften.

3 Place the dried fruit in an ovenproof dish, add the rhubarb and the cooking liquid and gently stir.

4 Cover the dish and bake for 20–25 minutes until the fruit has softened.

5 Serve warm or chilled with a dollop of yoghurt.

Each portion contains:

Energy	Fat	Saturates	Sugars	Salt
1472kJ 347kcals	0.7g	0.2g	79.1g	0.17g
18%	1%	1%	88%	3%

Of your reference intake

SUPER BERRY, CINNAMON AND HONEY GRANOLA

Serves 8 | Prep time: 10 minutes | Cook time: 10 minutes

STUFF YOU'LL NEED

150g/1¾ cups wholegrain rolled oats

50g/⅓ cup flaked almonds

50g/⅓ cup pumpkin seeds

25g/⅛ cup sunflower seeds

15g/⅛ cup sesame seeds

50g/¼ cup dried cranberries

50g/¼ cup dried blueberries

25g/⅛ cup Demerara sugar

1 tsp ground cinnamon

3 tbsp Fairtrade clear honey

3 tbsp vegetable oil

GET STUCK IN

1 Preheat the oven to 170°C/330°F/gas 3.

2 In a bowl, mix the oats, almonds, seeds and berries.

3 Heat the sugar, cinnamon, honey and oil together in a small pan. Stir until smooth, then pour on to the oat mixture. Mix well.

4 Tip the mixture into a large roasting tin. Bake for 10 minutes, stir well and then bake for a further 10 minutes or until golden, crisp and forming lumps. Leave to cool. Store in an airtight container for up to 10 days.

5 Serve granola in a bowl with fresh milk.

Each portion contains:

Energy	Fat	Saturates	Sugars	Salt
1056kJ 253kcals	15.3g	1.8g	6.2g	0.01g
13%	22%	9%	7%	0%

Of your reference intake

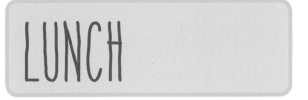

We all know that it's tough to get exactly what you want at lunchtimes. Shop-bought sandwiches are expensive and quite often sadly lacking in content and nutrients. Buy some good plastic tubs and take your own lunch in. It will be tastier, cheaper and everyone will be jealous!

HEARTY CHICKEN AND PASTA SOUP

Serves 4 | Prep time: 10 minutes | Cook time: 30 minutes

STUFF YOU'LL NEED

1 tbsp vegetable oil

1 large onion, finely chopped

1 or 2 leeks, sliced and soaked

3 sticks of celery, sliced

2 medium carrots

2 tsp mixed herbs

2–3 chicken stock cubes, made up with 1–1.5 litres/4¼–6½ cups boiling water

360g/13oz roasted chicken thighs

100g/3½oz pasta shells for soup

50g/½ cup frozen peas

Sea salt and freshly ground black pepper

GET STUCK IN

1 Heat the oil in a large saucepan over a medium heat and fry the chopped onion and sliced leeks for about 5 minutes, or until softened.

2 Add the sliced celery, carrots, mixed herbs and stock and bring to the boil.

3 Remove the skin from the chicken thighs and strip the chicken meat from the bone. Add the meat and pasta to the soup and stir.

4 Turn down the heat and simmer for 10–15 minutes or until the vegetables and pasta are cooked through. Just before serving add the peas and season to taste.

Each portion contains:

Energy	Fat	Saturates	Sugars	Salt
1213kJ 289kcals	9.0g	1.7g	8.3g	1.1g
14%	13%	8%	9%	18%

Of your reference intake

ROASTED PEPPERS WITH GOAT'S CHEESE

Serves 4 | Prep time: 20 minutes | Cook time: 25 minutes

STUFF YOU'LL NEED

4 red pimento peppers

Sea salt and freshly ground black pepper

50ml/3½ tbsp extra virgin olive oil

200g/⁷/₈ cup goat's cheese

200g/⁷/₈ cup soft cream cheese

2 cloves garlic

1 tbsp thyme leaves

Salt and freshly ground black pepper

100g/¾ cup hazelnuts, toasted and crushed

85g/3½oz salad leaves

150g/5¼oz baby spinach

150g/5¼oz baby red chard

50g/1¾oz flat leaf parsley

Vinaigrette (see page 152)

GET STUCK IN

1 Preheat the oven to 220°C/425°F/gas 7.

2 Cut the peppers in half and remove all of the seeds. Place on a baking tray and season with salt and pepper then drizzle with olive oil. Bake in the oven until lightly roasted.

3 Put the goat's cheese, cream cheese, garlic, thyme, salt and pepper in a food processor and blitz until smooth. Spoon this mix into the peppers and sprinkle with the hazelnuts. Place on a baking tray ready to be rebaked.

4 Wash the leaves and herbs then dry with kitchen paper. Put the peppers back in the oven, toss the leaves in the dressing and arrange on the plate. Place two peppers on each salad and drizzle some dressing around the edge.

Each portion contains:

Energy	Fat	Saturates	Sugars	Salt
2565kJ 619kcals	51.4g	18.5g	11.0g	3.1g
31%	73%	92%	12%	52%

Of your reference intake

AVOCADO AND PASTA SALAD WITH FLAXSEED

Serves 4 | Prep time: 10 minutes | Cook time: 10 minutes

STUFF YOU'LL NEED

200g/7oz penne pasta

½ clove garlic

1 large chilli

½ red onion

½ tsp Dijon mustard

2 limes, zested and juiced

20ml/1½ tbsp sherry vinegar (can be replaced with white wine)

100ml/7 tbsp hempseed oil (can be replaced with extra virgin olive oil)

1 ripe avocado

1 tbsp toasted flaxseed, crushed

Salt and freshly ground black pepper

1 handful of fresh basil leaves

GET STUCK IN

1 Cook the pasta according to the packet's instructions. Drain and place under running water until completely cold. Drain again in a colander.

2 Crush the garlic and finely slice the chilli and red onion. Mix together with the mustard, lime zest and juice and vinegar. Whisk in the oil and pour over the pasta.

3 When ready to serve, peel and stone the avocado. Dice relatively small and mix well into the pasta along with the flaxseed. Don't worry if it breaks up – it's meant to.

4 Season to taste and serve immediately with torn basil leaves on top.

Each portion contains:

Energy	Fat	Saturates	Sugars	Salt
1940kJ 462kcals	35.0g	5.6g	2.3g	0.4g
23%	50%	28%	3%	7%

Of your reference intake

CARROT, COCONUT AND ALMOND SOUP

Serves 4 | Prep time: 15 minutes | Cook time: 1 hour

STUFF YOU'LL NEED

50g/3½ tbsp unsalted butter

Dash of olive oil

600g/1lb 5oz carrot, chopped

½ large white onion, chopped

½ stick of celery, chopped

1 clove garlic, crushed

6 tbsp ground almonds

1 litre/4¼ cups vegetable stock

1 x 400ml/14fl oz tin coconut milk

½ lemon, juiced

Sea salt and freshly ground black pepper

3 tbsp chopped coriander

GET STUCK IN

1 Place the butter and oil in a heavy pan and allow to melt. Add all the vegetables and lightly sauté ensuring there is no colour. Cover and allow to steam for 5 minutes.

2 Add the ground almonds to the vegetables and mix well. Allow to toast lightly and then slowly add the warm stock, bring to the boil then turn down the heat and simmer until the carrots are soft enough to blitz.

3 Add the coconut milk to the pan and blitz until smooth, then pass through a fine sieve.

4 Add the lemon juice and season with salt and pepper to taste.

5 To serve, pour into soup bowls and garnish with coriander.

Each portion contains:

Energy	Fat	Saturates	Sugars	Salt
1121kJ 267kcals	19.1g	7.5g	17.6g	1.7g
13%	27%	38%	20%	28%

Of your reference intake

BEETROOT, FETA AND WALNUT SALAD

Serves 2 | Prep time: 5 minutes | Cook time: 5 minutes

STUFF YOU'LL NEED

4 fresh or vacuum-packed beetroots

2 tsp walnut oil

1 tsp white wine vinegar

½ tsp grain mustard

100g/3½oz green beans

1 bag of mixed salad leaves

50g/½ cup feta cheese

25g/¼ cup toasted walnuts

GET STUCK IN

1 Cut the beetroots into quarters and toss them in the walnut oil, white wine vinegar and grain mustard. Set aside.

2 Boil or steam the green beans for around 4 minutes, cool and then mix into the salad leaves. Arrange on 2 plates, add slices of the beetroot and crumble over the feta cheese and toasted walnuts.

Each portion contains:

Energy	Fat	Saturates	Sugars	Salt
1209kJ 292kcals	20.6g	5.2g	15g	1.2g
15%	29%	26%	15%	20%

Of your reference intake

DINNER

Dinner is a great time to communicate with your flatmates, friends and family. Cook together, share the cost, have a chat and do the washing up together!

CHEF'S RISOTTO WITH PEAS AND MINT

Serves 6 | Prep time: 10 minutes | Cook time: 30 minutes

STUFF YOU'LL NEED

Approx. 1.1 litres/4¼ cups stock (chicken, fish or vegetable as appropriate, see pages 60-2)

2 tbsp olive oil

1 knob of butter

1 large onion, finely chopped

2 cloves garlic, finely chopped

½ head of celery, finely chopped

400g/2 cups risotto rice

2 glasses dry white wine

Sea salt and freshly ground black pepper

100g/¾ cup defrosted peas

70g/¹⁄₃ cup butter

50g/⅓ cup freshly grated Parmesan cheese

4 sprigs fresh mint, chopped at the last minute

Note: add your own flavours such as mushrooms, peppers and asparagus.

GET STUCK IN

1 Heat the stock. In a separate pan, heat the olive oil and butter. Add the onions, garlic and celery and fry very slowly for about 15 minutes without colouring. When the vegetables have softened, add the rice and turn up the heat.

2 The rice will now begin to lightly fry, so keep stirring it. After a minute it will look slightly translucent. Add the wine and keep stirring – it will smell fantastic. Any harsh alcohol flavours will evaporate and leave the rice with a tasty essence.

3 When the rice has absorbed the wine, add your first ladle of hot stock and a good pinch of salt. Turn down the heat to a simmer so the rice doesn't cook too quickly on the outside. Keep adding ladlefuls of stock, stirring and almost massaging the creamy starch out of the rice. Allow each ladleful to be absorbed before adding the next. This will take around 15 minutes. Taste the rice – is it cooked?

4 Carry on adding stock until the rice is soft but with a slight bite. Don't forget to check the seasoning carefully. If you run out of stock before the rice is cooked, add some boiling water. Then add the defrosted peas and mix in well.

5 Remove from the heat and add the butter, Parmesan and mint. Stir well. Place a lid on the pan and allow to sit for 2 minutes. This is the most important part of making the perfect risotto, as this is when it becomes outrageously creamy and oozy like it should be. Eat it as soon as possible while the risotto retains its beautiful texture.

Each portion contains:

Energy	Fat	Saturates	Sugars	Salt
1084kJ 258kcals	16.6g	10.2g	3.0g	1.3g
13%	24%	51%	3%	22%

Of your reference intake

SEARED SALMON WITH SOY GREENS

Serves 2 | Prep time: 15 minutes | Cook time: 20 minutes

STUFF YOU'LL NEED

2 salmon fillets, skin on

Sea salt and freshly ground black pepper

2 tbsp plain flour, to dust

1 tbsp sunflower oil

150g/5¼oz bok choy, quartered

1 fresh red chilli, deseeded and finely diced

Finely grated zest and juice of ½ lime

1 tbsp Japanese soy sauce (Kikkoman's)

½ tbsp Thai fish sauce (optional)

150ml/²/₃ cup black bean sauce

120ml/½ cup marinated fish/vegetable stock

2 tbsp chopped fresh coriander

lime wedges, to serve

GET STUCK IN

1 Season the salmon fillets with salt and pepper and dust with flour. Heat a non-stick pan and add a dash of sunflower oil. Put the salmon fillets skin-side down in the pan (press down the fillets, this will prevent any shrinking). Sear the salmon for 3–4 minutes. The skin should be crisp and the light pinkness of the fish creeping up to the halfway point as it cooks.

2 Turn it over for a further 2 minutes then remove from the heat. Lift the fish out of the pan and season with a little salt and pepper. Leave to rest whilst you cook the bok choy.

3 To cook the bok choy, add 1 tablespoon of oil to a pan or wok and stir-fry the leaves for a few minutes until wilted. Add the chilli, lime zest, soy sauce, fish sauce and stir in the black bean sauce, then add the fish stock. Season with black pepper and cook for a few minutes. Add the lime juice and chopped coriander and bring to the boil, then taste. Remove from the heat and keep warm.

4 To serve, heap a mound of bok choy in the centre of shallow bowls or plates and spoon the sauce around, add a wedge of lime and place the salmon fillets on top.

Each portion contains:

Energy	Fat	Saturates	Sugars	Salt
1672kJ 398kcals	19.5g	2.7g	10.1g	8.2g
20%	28%	14%	11%	137%

Of your reference intake

GARLIC ROASTED CHICKEN WITH ROASTED CARROTS, POTATOES AND GRAVY

Serves 4 | Prep time: 30 minutes | Cook time: 1 hour 45 minutes

STUFF YOU'LL NEED

1.5kg/3lb 5oz organic free-range chicken

1 lemon, halved

1 bulb garlic, sliced in half through the cloves

2 sprigs fresh thyme (one for inside and one for outside)

110g/½ cup salted butter plus 25g/¹⁄₈ cup salted butter, softened, for smearing

500g/1lb 2oz carrots, cut in half lengthways

2 red onions, quartered

1 stick of celery, diced

½ onion, diced

½ leek, diced

1 carrot, diced

2 twigs fresh tarragon stalks and leaves

1 heaped tbsp plain flour

1 glass white wine

500ml/2 cups chicken stock (see page 60)

GET STUCK IN

1 Preheat the oven to 180°C/350°F/gas 4.

2 To prepare the chicken for roasting, remove the giblets from inside the bird if there are any. Take half of the bulb of garlic and rub over the skin of the chicken. Squeeze the lemon juice over the bird and put the squeezed half inside the body cavity with the garlic, thyme and 110g/½ cup butter.

3 Spread the softened butter all over the bird, then sprinkle with more thyme.

4 Put the chicken in a roasting tin with the carrots and onions and put it into the oven to roast for 1¼–1½ hours, basting with the juices in the tin from time to time. To test if the chicken is cooked, pierce the thigh with the tip of a sharp knife; when the chicken is cooked the juices will run clear.

5 When the chicken has finished cooking, put it on a carving board and set aside in a warm place to rest for 15 minutes. This helps to relax the meat, making it more tender and moist.

6 Remove the carrots and onions and set these aside somewhere warm.

7 Skim off some of the fat from the juices in the tin. Set the tin over a medium heat, add the diced vegetables and tarragon stalks and cook until softened. Dust with the flour and mix well. When the flour is combined, cook for a couple of minutes and add the wine. Bring to the boil and reduce by half. Add the stock and allow to reduce in volume by one-third. Pass through a sieve into a saucepan, add a squeeze of lemon juice and keep hot. Add the chopped tarragon leaves just before serving.

8 Put the chicken in the middle of the table and divide among hot plates. Serve with the roast carrots, onions and roast potatoes smothered in lots of gravy!

Each portion contains:

Energy	Fat	Saturates	Sugars	Salt
4666kJ **1111kcals**	**77.4g**	**30.1g**	**16.6g**	**1.5g**
56%	**111%**	**150%**	**18%**	**25%**

Of your reference intake

CHICKEN AND VEGETABLE STIR-FRY WITH NOODLES

Serves 4 | Prep time: 10 minutes | Cook time: 10 minutes

STUFF YOU'LL NEED

250g/9oz egg noodles

4 tbsp vegetable oil

3 tbsp sesame oil

1 clove garlic, chopped

½ red pepper, deseeded and sliced

½ yellow pepper, deseeded and sliced

½ green pepper, deseeded and sliced

2 carrots, sliced into strips

2 sticks of celery, sliced

200g/7oz beansprouts

2 skinless, boneless chicken breasts, cut on the diagonal into strips 1cm/⅓in wide

3 tbsp sesame seeds, toasted

1 tbsp dark soy sauce

3 tbsp oyster sauce

GET STUCK IN

1 Cook the noodles in a large pan of boiling water for 2–3 minutes until soft.

2 Once the noodles are cooked, drain and return to the saucepan. Toss well in 1 tablespoon of vegetable oil and set aside. Cover with a tea towel.

3 Heat a wok until very hot and then add 2 tablespoons of vegetable and sesame oil. Add the garlic after 30 seconds. Toss in the sliced peppers and carrots and stir-fry for another 30 seconds, then add the sliced celery and beansprouts. Add a splash of soy sauce and then take out of the wok and set to one side.

4 Add the remaining vegetable and sesame oil to the pan. Add the chicken and stir-fry for 3 minutes or until it takes on a golden colour. When the chicken is ready put the vegetables back in to the wok with the noodles and the toasted sesame seeds. Stir in the soy sauce and oyster sauce. Cook for 1 minute, stirring constantly and serve immediately.

Each portion contains:

Energy	Fat	Saturates	Sugars	Salt
1523kJ	15.5g	1.5g	5.3g	2.13g
378kcals				
18%	22%	8%	6%	36%

Of your reference intake

HEALTHY LAMB BURGER

Serves 4 | Prep time: 30 minutes | Cook time: 10–20 minutes

STUFF YOU'LL NEED

1 onion, very finely chopped or grated

1 free-range egg, beaten

450g/1lb minced lamb, extra lean

1 stick of celery, very finely chopped

1 tbsp tomato purée

2 tbsp mint

2 tbsp Worcestershire sauce

60g/1 cup fresh breadcrumbs

1 tbsp plain flour, for dusting

For the tzatziki

120ml/½ cup yoghurt

¼ cucumber, grated and squeezed dry

1 clove garlic, finely grated

Salt and freshly ground black pepper

To serve

8 small soft wholemeal buns

150g/5¼oz feta cheese, crumbled (optional)

Salad

GET STUCK IN

1 Place the onion, egg, lamb, celery, tomato purée, mint, Worcestershire sauce and breadcrumbs in a large bowl and mix thoroughly with your hands until well combined.

2 Divide the mixture into eight and form each portion into a ball. Using your hands, press the mixture together firmly. Turn each ball onto a lightly floured surface and press down with the palm of your hand to form burgers.

3 Grill or barbecue for 5–8 minutes on each side or until cooked through.

4 Whilst they are cooking, make the tzatziki. Combine the yoghurt, squeezed cucumber and garlic, stir well and season to taste.

5 Serve with wholemeal bread rolls, crumbled feta, if you like, tzatziki and salad.

Each portion contains:

Energy	Fat	Saturates	Sugars	Salt
1390kJ **331kcals**	**19.5g**	**8.1g**	**3.9g**	**0.8g**
17%	28%	40%	4%	13%

Of your reference intake

PUDDINGS

I cannot finish a meal without something sweet. I don't know why, it's just part of my make-up. These puds are good for you, although they do contain sugar, so keep the portion sizes down to ample but not too much. Take your time eating and they'll satisfy and reward you after a long day.

ESPRESSO NECTARINES

Serves: 4 | Prep time: 5 minutes | Cook time: 10 minutes

STUFF YOU'LL NEED

750ml/3 cups orange juice

4 tbsp sugar

2 shots of espresso or 4 tsp instant coffee

4 ripe nectarines

1 orange

Vanilla ice cream, to serve

GET STUCK IN

1 Pour the orange juice and sugar into a medium pan and bring to the boil. Add the coffee – fresh espresso tastes a bit better but it doesn't matter.

2 Cut the nectarines into two, removing the stone. Slice the orange into 8 thin slices leaving the skin on. Gently lower the nectarines and the orange slices into the orange juice.

3 Poach the nectarines for 3–4 minutes. To test whether they are cooked, insert a small knife, it should meet with little resistance. Transfer the fruit and juice to a bowl to cool at room temperature. Cover and refrigerate for at least 3 hours to let the flavours develop.

4 To serve, lay the orange slices out and place the nectarines on and around them. Serve with scoops of vanilla ice cream.

Each portion contains:

Energy	Fat	Saturates	Sugars	Salt
677kJ 159kcals	0.4g	0g	35.8g	0.1g
8%	1%	0%	40%	2%

Of your reference intake

ORANGE AND ROSEHIP YOGHURT SORBET

Serves 4 | Prep time: 30 minutes | Cook time: 5 minutes | Churn time: 30 minutes–1 hour

STUFF YOU'LL NEED

350ml/1½ cups orange juice (made up of at least 2 fresh oranges – keep the orange shells for serving)

225g/1 cup caster sugar

3 tbsp liquid glucose

3 rosehip tea bags cut open

300ml/1¼ cups natural yoghurt

100ml/7 tbsp fromage frais

GET STUCK IN

1 Pour the orange juice into a heavy saucepan. Add the sugar, liquid glucose and rosehip tea leaves and place over a low heat. Stir occasionally until the sugar has dissolved, then increase the heat and boil for 3–4 minutes. Remove from the heat and cool completely.

2 Beat the yoghurt and fromage frais together in a bowl until smooth. Mix in the cooled syrup.

3 Pour the mixture into an ice-cream machine and churn until frozen and almost firm, then scoop the sorbet out into the halved orange shells and place in the freezer for several hours until firm

Note: if you do not have an ice-cream machine, freeze the mixture in a shallow container and beat with a fork several times during freezing.

Each portion contains:

Energy	Fat	Saturates	Sugars	Salt
1587kJ	**2.3g**	**1.5g**	**75.4g**	**0.24g**
374kcals				
19%	3%	8%	84%	4%

Of your reference intake

FRUIT SALAD WITH ELDERFLOWER MERINGUES

Serves: 4 | Prep time: 1–2 hours | Cook time: 1½ hours

STUFF YOU'LL NEED

200g/1⅓ cups strawberries, halved

50g/⅓ cup pomegranate seeds

150g/1¼ cups blueberries

100g/3½oz melon, cubed

100g/3½oz pineapple, cubed

5 tbsp elderflower cordial

For the meringues

3 egg whites

175g/¾ cup caster sugar

10ml/2 tsp elderflower cordial

200ml/¾ cup whipping cream

GET STUCK IN

1 Preheat the oven to 110°C/230°F/gas ½.

2 Soak all the fruit in the elderflower cordial for at least 1 hour.

3 Whisk the egg whites until firm, carry on whisking, adding 1 tablespoon of sugar at a time until half of the sugar has been used. Fold in the remaining sugar together with the elderflower cordial.

4 Using a tablespoon dipped in warm water, spoon the mixture into small rounds onto metal trays lined with non-stick paper.

5 Lightly bake the meringues in the oven for 1 hour 40 minutes or until crisp, then arrange them on a wire rack to cool.

6 If piping cream inside, then whip the cream until it forms soft peaks and use it to sandwich together pairs of meringue shells. Spoon the fruit into a glass and spoon over a bit of the elderflower cordial in which you marinated the fruit.

7 Serve with a little whipped cream.

Note: please feel free to add any fruit you love.

Each portion contains:

Energy	Fat	Saturates	Sugars	Salt
1779kJ 424kcals	20.5g	12.6g	58.9g	0.16g
21%	29%	63%	62%	2%

Of your reference intake

BLUEBERRY JELLY WITH PROSECCO TOPPED WITH GREEK YOGHURT AND HONEY

Serves 6 | Prep time: 15 minutes | Cook time: 5 minutes

STUFF YOU'LL NEED

200g/1 cup caster sugar

500ml/2 cups prosecco

3 sheets gelatine

800g/6½ cups blueberries

300ml/1¼ cups Greek yoghurt

1½ tbsp honey

50g/⅓ cup flaked almonds, toasted

GET STUCK IN

1 In a pan over a low heat, dissolve the caster sugar in half the prosecco. Bring to the boil and boil for 3–4 minutes.

2 Meanwhile place the gelatine in a bowl of cold tap water to soften. This takes a few minutes. When soft, squeeze out and reserve in a small bowl.

3 Take the sugar syrup off the heat and stir in the reserved gelatine. Make sure it is well dissolved. Leave to cool and then mix in the remaining prosecco.

4 Divide the blueberries among six glasses. Pour in enough syrup to cover the blueberries and chill for a few hours. Mix the yoghurt and honey together, then serve each jelly with a small dollop of yoghurt sprinkled with toasted almonds.

Each portion contains:

Energy	Fat	Saturates	Sugars	Salt
1479kJ	9.8g	3.8g	43.7g	0.2g
352kcals				
18%	14%	19%	49%	3%

Of your reference intake

GARDEN GINGER AND RHUBARB CRUMBLE

Serves 4-6 | Prep time: 20 minutes | Cook time: 35 minutes

STUFF YOU'LL NEED

10 rhubarb stalks, trimmed and sliced into 5cm/2in chunks

1 tbsp water

2-3 tbsp caster sugar

1 tbsp stem ginger in syrup, chopped

Greek yoghurt, to serve

For the crumble

60g/¼ cup butter, softened

80g/⅔ cup plain flour

60g/¼ cup Demerara sugar

60g/2oz granola

GET STUCK IN

1 Preheat the oven to 180°C/350°F/gas 4.

2 To make the crumble, combine the butter and flour and rub with your fingers until the mixture resembles breadcrumbs. Add the sugar and granola and mix well.

3 Place on an oven tray and bake for 15 minutes or until golden brown. Stir halfway through.

4 Place the rhubarb chunks in a shallow roasting pan, sprinkle with the water and the caster sugar. Bake for 10 minutes. Remove from the oven and sprinkle with the ginger.

5 Tip the rhubarb mixture into a baking dish of about 4cm/1½in deep. Sprinkle the crumble evenly over the rhubarb. Bake for 10 minutes until warmed through and golden.

6 Allow to cool slightly before serving. Serve with dollops of Greek yoghurt.

Each portion contains:

Energy	Fat	Saturates	Sugars	Salt
1612kJ 381kcals	15.1g	8.1g	36.7g	0.28g
19%	22%	41%	41%	4%

Of your reference intake

CHOCOLATE POT WITH ORANGE MARMALADE SALSA

Serves: 4 | Prep time: 30 minutes | Cook time: 10 minutes

STUFF YOU'LL NEED

For the salsa

2 oranges, zested and segmented

200g/1 cup caster sugar

100ml/7 tbsp water

4 heads of lavender flowers (fresh or dried)

1 tbsp orange marmalade

For the chocolate pot

250ml/1 cup double cream

½ vanilla pod, cut in half and seeds scraped out

150g/5¼oz dark chocolate

100g/½ cup caster sugar

2 large egg yolks

50g/3½ tbsp cold, unsalted butter, diced

GET STUCK IN!

1 For the salsa, peel off the zest from the oranges then cut them into fine shreds.

2 Remove any pith from the outer edge of the orange, segment and dice the flesh.

3 Place the sugar and water in a pan and bring to the boil, stirring occasionally until the sugar is dissolved, then cook for a further 2–3 minutes. Remove from the heat and allow to cool.

4 Mix the segmented orange, lavender and marmalade with the syrup; set aside and allow to infuse.

5 For the chocolate pot: in a heavy pan, heat the cream and vanilla pod and seeds until nearly boiling. Set aside for 1 minute before removing the vanilla pod and adding the chocolate.

6 In a separate bowl, mix the sugar and egg yolks until fully combined, then add them to the chocolate mix followed by the cold, diced butter.

7 Pour into the chosen serving dishes and place a small spoonful of salsa on top.

Each portion contains:

Energy	Fat	Saturates	Sugars	Salt
4140kJ 991kcals	60.7g	35.5g	111g	0.09g
50%	87%	178%	123%	1%

Of your reference intake

20 REASONS WHY YOU SHOULD KEEP COOKING

I hope that I have inspired you to start cooking. It's really simple. Food is lovely when it's fresh and not mucked about with too much. It can be quick and easy to prepare and really enjoyable, healthy and satisfying to provide for others.

I wrote this book not only to encourage you to start cooking but keep cooking. So here are 20 reasons to do so.

1 The advantage of knowing exactly what's in your food.

2 You won't have to decide between cheap takeaways that never taste as you thought they would.

3 It's easier to change your habits when cooking for yourself; you will also pick up ideas when you go to restaurants.

4 You can still make your favourite recipes, but using healthier substitutions; your meals will now be much tastier.

5 You can prevent food cravings and overeating.

6 You can bake people cakes and lovely things for their birthdays and make them very happy.

7 You'll be heathier without even trying, and can control the amount you eat and when you eat it.

8 Your friends will be so impressed, and they will be in awe of you forever.

9 Your colleagues at work will love you bringing in goodies and you'll get promoted, yeah!

10 You'll save money, a load of money.

11 You will develop your knife skills and look professional at dinner parties.

12 Everyone loves a good cook. You'll get loads of dates.

13 You will be able to satisfy your every craving.

14 You can make anything once you start cooking, when you see how easy it really is.

15 You can help reduce your risk of certain diseases, such as diabetes and heart disease.

16 You can plan healthy meals ahead including snacks to avoid eating an unhealthy diet.

17 You will pass good cooking on to your family.

18 You can share the fun of buying, preparing, eating and clearing up together.

19 Once you start cooking your will have much more motivation to change other parts of your life.

20 Come on, cooking is cool.

WEIGHTS AND MEASURES

Use this helpful guide to find baking and cooking conversions between metric, imperial and US cup measures.

Convert carefully

For most home cooks, an extra gram or two of an ingredient won't make much of a difference. Once you start working with larger quantities, however, precision counts: an incorrect measurement can throw off a ratio and ruin a recipe. Proper ingredient measurements are especially important in baking. If you're working with larger quantities, especially in baking, seek out a precise conversion tool on the internet, or use a search engine to convert between metric and imperial.

Liquids

When measuring liquid, cooking measurements are quite straightforward:

Metric	Imperial	US cups
250ml	8fl oz	1 cup
180ml	6fl oz	¾ cup
150ml	5fl oz	$2/_3$ cup
120ml	4fl oz	½ cup
75ml	2½fl oz	$1/_3$ cup
60ml	2fl oz	¼ cup
30ml	1fl oz	$1/_8$ cup
15ml	½fl oz	1 tablespoon

Solids

Check this chart for basic imperial to metric conversions:

½oz	15g
1oz	30g
2oz	60g
3oz	90g
4oz	110g
5oz	140g
6oz	170g
7oz	200g
8oz	225g
9oz	255g
10oz	280g
11oz	310g
12oz	340g
13oz	370g
14oz	400g
15oz	425g
1lb	450g

Spoons!

Ever stop to wonder about teaspoons, dessertspoons and tablespoons? Here are their metric equivalents.
But first:
1 dessertspoon = 2 teaspoons
3 teaspoons = 1 tablespoon

1 teaspoon	5ml
2 teaspoons	10ml
1 tablespoon	15ml
2 tablespoons	30ml
3 tablespoons	45ml
4 tablespoons	60ml
5 tablespoons	75ml
6 tablespoons	90ml
7 tablespoons	105ml

Tablespoons can be easily used to convert dry (and wet) ingredients to/ from US cups. Here's a simple conversion chart:

Tablespoons to US cups

1 tablespoon	$^1/_{16}$ cup
2 tablespoons	$^1/_8$ cup
4 tablespoons	¼ cup
5 tablespoons	$^1/_3$ cup
8 tablespoons	½ cup
10 tablespoons	$^2/_3$ cup
12 tablespoons	¾ cup
16 tablespoons	1 cup

Weight of common ingredients

Found a recipe in US cups? Keep in mind a cup of butter weighs much more than a cup of flour! Use this chart to convert common ingredients between cups, metric and imperial:

Plain flour and icing sugar

US cups	Metric	Imperial
$^1/_8$ cup	15g	½oz
¼ cup	30g	1oz
$^1/_3$ cup	40g	1½oz
½ cup	65g	2¼oz
$^2/_3$ cup	85g	3oz
¾ cup	95g	3¼oz
1 cup	125g	4½oz

Sugar (caster and granulated)

US cups	Metric	Imperial
$^1/_8$ cup	25g	1oz
¼ cup	50g	1¾oz
$^1/_3$ cup	70g	2¼oz
½ cup	100g	3½oz
$^2/_3$ cup	135g	4¾oz
¾ cup	150g	5¼oz
1 cup	200g	7oz

Porridge oats

US cups	Metric	Imperial
$^1/_8$ cup	10g	$^1/_3$oz
¼ cup	20g	¾oz
$^1/_3$ cup	30g	1oz
½ cup	45g	1½oz
¾ cup	60g	2¼oz
1 cup	85g	3oz

Brown soft sugar

US cups	Metric	Imperial
$^1/_8$ cup	25g	1oz
¼ cup	55g	2oz
$^1/_3$ cup	75g	2½oz
½ cup	110g	4oz
$^2/_3$ cup	150g	5oz
¾ cup	170g	6oz
1 cup	220g	7¾oz

Honey, treacle and syrup

US cups	Metric	Imperial
$^1/_8$ cup	45g	1½oz
¼ cup	85g	3oz
$^1/_3$ cup	110g	4oz
½ cup	170g	6oz
$^2/_3$ cup	225g	8oz
¾ cup	250g	9oz
1 cup	340g	12oz

Butter and margarine

US cups	Metric	Imperial
$^1/_8$ cup	25g	1oz
¼ cup	60g	2oz
$^1/_3$ cup	75g	3oz
½ cup	110g	4oz
$^2/_3$ cup	150g	5¼oz
¾ cup	180g	6¼oz
1 cup	225g	8oz

Quick conversions

For other common ingredients, here are some quick conversions from US cups to metric:

1 cup chocolate chips = 150g

1 cup cocoa powder = 125g

1 cup chopped walnuts or pecans = 125g

1 cup walnut or pecan halves = 100g

1 cup desiccated coconut = 75g

1 tablespoon baking powder = 15g

1 tablespoon salt = 18g

1 cup grated Cheddar cheese = 120g

1 cup grated Parmesan cheese = 80g

1 cup dried breadcrumbs = 120g

1 cup couscous = 175g

1 cup lentils = 190g

1 cup sultanas or raisins = 170g

RECIPE INDEX

Dedicated to my parents; your food empowered me.

And for lovely, beautiful Tracey.

You've taught me that simple food cooked with love, care and attention
is a constant education.

With thanks to:

Leon Seraphin at Beyond Food for your countless kitchen sessions using my recipes.

Stuart Hounslow for your amazing hand-drawn illustrations.

Hilda Mulrooney and the nutritional students at Kingston University for helping me to
evaluate the recipes.

Carey Smith, Samantha Crisp & Jo Whitehead at Penguin Random House for the support.

All at Beyond Food and Brigade for supporting this adventure and the change
it may provide.